CW01020791

# THE
# GHOST
# LAKE

Also by Wendy Pratt

*Gifts the Mole Gave Me*
*When I Think of My Body as a Horse*
*Blackbird Singing at Dusk*

# THE GHOST LAKE

W E N D Y   P R A T T

THE BOROUGH PRESS

The Borough Press
An imprint of HarperCollins*Publishers* Ltd
1 London Bridge Street
London SE1 9GF

www.harpercollins.co.uk

HarperCollins*Publishers*
Macken House,
39/40 Mayor Street Upper,
Dublin 1
D01 C9W8
Ireland

First published by HarperCollins*Publishers* Ltd 2024

1

A catalogue record for this book is available from the British Library.

ISBN: 978-0-00-863737-8

Typeset by Palimpsest Book Production Ltd, Falkirk, Stirlingshire

Printed and bound in the UK using 100% Renewable Electricity
by CPI Group (UK) Ltd

In memory of my dad, Dave Burn,
and for Matilda, always.

# Contents

MOORS

Seamer
Beacon

Woodlands
Cemetery

Crossgates

Seamer

Eastfield

Site of
Flixton Island

Star Carr
Mesolithic
Site

*Paleolake*

Staxton

Spital Farm

Probable site of
Carman's Spital

THE

*arborough*

NORTH SEA

Cayton

Site of
o Name Hill

RIVER HERTFORD

*lixton*

Flixton

Folkton

To Hunmanby

To Folkton Drums
Neolithic Burial Site

VOLDS

# CHAPTER ONE

# The Lake People

A buzzard is drifting across the darkening sky; the blunt tail and V-shape of its wings silhouetted against the dusk. I have the car windows down, radio switched off, enjoying the sounds of the valley and the rich smell of cow dung and soil, the smell of spring. Sparrows chatter in hedgerows as I pass, and a soft wind is blowing, bending the grasses, shimmying the bullrushes of the small ponds and pools that never quite dry up.

I am driving across an agricultural landscape of flat, green fields, electric fences, hawthorn hedges and beech copses, a nondescript valley that holds a secret: here is where a glacial lake once was. Paleolake Flixton; an extinct lake, now just a watermark on the land, visible only when the mist rises and fills it, like a bowl with milk, or in the deep black of the valley night, when the lights of the surrounding villages illuminate the lake border. As I drive, I imagine myself slipping into the ancient waters, the weight of my existence lifting away.

There are few signs of human habitation on the lake site

1

itself. Most of it is too marshy and wet to build houses on, even though the lake – once four kilometres across and eight metres deep in places – has been gone for a thousand years. However, some small fields have farming equipment stored in them. One field I pass regularly has what looks like a roundhouse, half constructed, in the corner. It is a circle of timber posts with timber struts that form a conical roof. Each time I see it I think of the first dwelling places that the people who settled here after the glaciers receded used; the Mesolithic roundhouses found at the archaeological site of Star Carr, on the opposite end of the lake. I think of the timber post holes and the circle of the foot-flattened inner, the soot from a fire put out eleven thousand years ago.

The Star Carr people were hunter-gatherers, nomads whose survival depended on hunting, fishing and gathering wild plants. The Mesolithic people did not farm. They were the people who came before the Neolithic, farming people who would later inhabit the valley. The Mesolithic community of Star Carr came to the lake at certain times of year and left at others, presumably following migrating animals. But they kept returning, year after year. They deposited the markers of their lives in the lake itself, leaving animal parts, flints, tools and deer skull headdresses in the water in what are widely accepted as ritualistic gestures.

I imagine the Star Carr people as people who showed reverence towards the animals of this place, aware of their own connection to, and reliance on, nature. These were people whose lives rested on how they connected to this landscape, on the lake itself, and their belonging is entwined with their returning, over and over, for hundreds of years, to the same place, the same roundhouses, the same interiors flattened by their own ancestors' feet. The smoky light, the stutter of geese skirting the water as they returned from their travels, the red deer in the woods and forests, a sense of belonging, maybe even of home.

The lake site is sizeable. I live at the eastern end of it, my mum lives on the western side, and around its edges are a series of roads passing through villages and across carrland. Some days I drive out deliberately to feel for its shape, to see the light change over the surface of the flat fields. To remind myself of my own life lying over it like a dust sheet. I set off from my tiny village, with its red pantiled roofs and corrugated iron church, and head inland, through the village of Cayton, where my dad's body lay in the funeral home, and the housing estate of Eastfield where I went to secondary school. I drive past the Crossgates estate where I grew up, past the boulder perched on its grass promontory – a boulder carried all the way from Cumbria in the belly of a glacier and left behind here when the glacier that carved the valley receded. I go on to Seamer, where my mum now lives, the mound of Seamer Beacon on the horizon; the road diverging, streaking up towards a Bronze Age burial site. Then through Seamer village, with the chapel I was married in, and out again, turning towards the Wolds and on, past the fields beneath which the Mesolithic site of Star Carr sleeps, then turning again towards the sea, navigating through Flixton and its long-lost islands, land of the Palaeolithic people, through the place once known as wolf land where a hospital stood to give travellers refuge, through Folkton with its Norman church, and the Neolithic children's grave where the Folkton Drums were found, a short walk away. I wind along the valley and turn north again, the lake to one side and the sea to the other, my back to my village and the place I know as home.

Today I have cut across the lake, taken the carr road. This is the only public road that traverses the site. It cuts through the footprint of the lake roughly two thirds across on the eastern side. This bisection of the lake has Cayton at one side and Folkton at the other, and in between is a flat expanse of land that was once the bottom of the lake, but now moves like water only because of wheatfields and long meadow grasses.

There are farm tracks that cross the carr; the wetland areas where the lake once was of course, and bridleways, sunken lanes and holloways down the valley sides, trade routes and dog walking paths and straggly foot-worn places of passage, but this is the only place I can drive out to as part of my everyday journeys. This is the only place I can feel the gravity of driving along the bottom of the lake. I feel centred here, like the central point of a compass. To the north is the North York Moors National Park, and the Dales and valleys and villages my family would visit in our old, battered camper van. To the east is the North Sea, Scarborough, Filey and Bridlington clinging onto the land, fishing boats clinking against each other in the harbours, cafés I worked in as a teenager, holiday flats we cleaned every weekend, the beach where I'd wander wide-eyed and hungover on a Saturday morning, the places I go fossil hunting and dog walking. To the south, the Yorkshire Wolds, those high chalk plateaus and valleys pocked with burial mounds and Iron Age forts. And to the west, the valley rolling on towards York, the edges closing and opening, rounded and smoothed from the glacier that ground its way into the landscape at the last ice age, leaving this deep, wide U-shape, the glacial runoff forming the Palaeolithic lake twelve thousand years ago. This is the place that I have been rooted to, have circled my whole life. The place that is in me, and the place that I am in, where I have lived and grown and been bereaved and been loved.

The River Hertford crossing the valley floor is rippling with the deep pink and dusky blue of evening. The lights in the surrounding villages are coming on, the taillights of cars are winding up the valley sides to the Wolds. I park in a layby near the waterworks: a set of concrete tubes, tubs and metal platforms nestled in among a clump of willow and birch trees. I like the intersection between this modern structure of piped and processed water and waste, and the long sweep of arable and pasture fields stretching out in front. Here there is a sense of time being a thin skin through which, if I press my face, I might see the Star Carr people, and on and on through all the other lake people: the Romans, Saxons, Vikings and Normans, through the industrialization of farming, the wartime bombing of the coastal towns and up to this point, up to this person – me – time lapping against my feet.

The lake is a place of transience and liminality. It has risen and waned, its people have left and come back, and new people have arrived. The original lake dwellers were nomadic, using the land and the lake for their own needs. At one point in the far-off past, this is what it was to exist. The Mesolithic people of Star Carr must have had a mutable sense of belonging and home. But I like to think that they had favourite places, and that this place was more than just somewhere to hunt red deer. The ritual deposits of hunting masks and the careful building of roundhouses have an edge of permanence. And in fact these houses *were* returned to, fixed and improved year on year. Perhaps 'home' for the Star Carr people was multiple, in the same way that we might revisit places, staying in the same hotel, returning to the same beach and feeling that ache of relief when we crest the hill and see the sea and feel transported to a different lifestyle, a different life, even for a few days, a few weeks – for the Star Carr people, a few months. That is a kind of belonging.

There's no genetic link between myself and the Star Carr people, or if there is, I wouldn't know it. I have no stamp of ownership on this place I call home. Perhaps the definition of 'home' itself is subjective, perhaps it is less physical, more emotional. But the landscape itself feels like my idea of home. It is the landscape that gives a sense of continuity to my life. In the same way that I look at the same sun that the Star Carr people looked at, I look at the same hills, the same slope of valley wall. I attach myself to the lake, the skyline of ridges and burial mounds, the patterns of tree plantations on the side of the valley walls. I feel embedded in the landscape, or the landscape feels embedded in me. I don't know how to split that away. I'm left wondering what the difference between *home* and a sense of *belonging* is. I wonder if there *is* a difference between the traveller arriving here and setting up camp, knowing they'll leave again, and me, who has lived here all my life.

In fact, I have never lived more than nineteen miles from the hospital where I was born, in Scarborough. That hospital later became a psychiatric hospital. I struggled so much with my mental health in my early to late twenties and later, after the death of my baby daughter, I ended up an outpatient there, like a circle being completed or a snake eating its own tail. I was born in Scarborough, but I lived on a housing estate on the edges of town. I grew up in a working-class household, in a place surrounded by fields and lanes.

We were poor but we did not live in poverty. 'Working class' and 'poverty' are not synonymous. It would be much easier to grasp the slippery and malleable definition of 'working class' if they were, but they're not. They can be, of course, but not always. I have never lived in poverty but, like most working-class people, I have seen poverty up close, in family and friends, and I have known the absolute fear of being two or three steps away from ruination at any one time.

My mum came from a council estate and a large, chaotic family. People knew of them in the town of Thirsk where she was born and raised. My dad, also from Thirsk, came from a long line of tenant farmers and farm labourers, but at fifteen he eschewed farming and became a Ringtons Tea van driver. Having learned to drive on a tractor aged seven or eight, he drove whatever he could when he left home. After the van came buses, courier cars and then buses again, with spells as a building labourer and a holiday flats owner. My dad wasn't a farmer, but he brought a farmer's mentality with him through life. He carried his closeness to nature under his skin. I grew up with nature as my backdrop, in the house martins nesting under the eaves, the toads in the pond, rabbits, foxes, curlews, crab apple trees, swathes of marshland and bogland, farms and farmers and a great blackness between villages.

My parents have always been aspirational. They wanted more than the hand they were dealt. My dad died in 2022, and the strangeness of grief is that you often discover so much more about a person after they die. I found out, while helping my mum write his eulogy, that he paid his mortgage off in twelve years, on a single-income household with three children. As a child I remember him coming into the house dead on his feet from twelve-hour shifts driving buses, dropping into a chair in front of the three-bar fire while we played with Lego round his feet. The Lego, incidentally, came from jumble sales and charity shops – we didn't get new stuff between birthdays and Christmas. None of the working-class families we knew did. I don't remember feeling like we were missing out, people who donated to charity seemed to be able to afford to give stuff away that was hardly used. I could never quite believe it when we came across the most sought-after Christmas craze at a jumble sale a year later, barely played with.

When my dad got a transfer to Scarborough with Ringtons, aged seventeen, he decided to embrace it, to leave the farm back in Thirsk and begin his own life here, in this valley. After a year or so my parents had scraped together the deposit for their little box house just outside Scarborough. Twelve years of back-breaking shifts later and he had paid off his mortgage. It never occurred to me then to question why this was so important to him, why the owning of his own home, the land that he stood on, was such an integral part of his plan. It's only now, after his death, that I seem to have perspective on his life, his motivations. How growing up a tenant farmer's son meant growing up dependent on the plans of the farm owner, which meant having less autonomy and less security.

The newbuild homes of my childhood were another liminal place: not a village, not a council estate, just a bunch of 1970s houses pushed into the valley. This was a place where on-the-up working-class people and what might be termed 'lower-middle-class' homeowners lived alongside each other. This was a place of middle managers and the self-employed, where our family seemed to stick out like a sore thumb. We were known for our scrap-heap cars that my dad bought cheap and fixed himself. There was always a ring of rust and a slick of oil on our driveway. We were skip raiders. We took the things our neighbours had thrown away and we reused them. We ate own brand and home-baked, and we lived in hand-me-downs and clothes from jumble sales. We had scraggly dogs and cats. My dad grew his own vegetables to save money. We had a make-do-and-mend mentality that some people looked down on. We would head out on a weekend in our rust bucket of a car/van/estate/whatever the cheap vehicle of the day was, and my dad would play bus driver, sweeping us onto the moors or onto the Wolds, taking us on a 'magical mystery tour'. Sometimes there would be sandwiches consumed in a layby. Sometimes we'd pull over at a stream running through the gorse and heather and go paddling. We'd head to half-hidden Roman roads and walk them barefoot, shifting roaming Swaledale sheep out of the way to get where we were going.

Looking back, there was a wildness to our family. We were always happiest scrubbing about in the dirt, wandering, getting lost. When we'd visit relatives in Thirsk, which we did every couple of weeks, we'd take detours into the countryside. My dad knew the roads so well he rarely needed a map. When we returned, we'd look for the signs of home in the landscape. I would feel then as I do now, the same drop in anxiety, a weight lifted off my shoulders, the familiarity of this place like a key that fitted the strange lock that I was.

I had grown up feeling at odds with the world. There was, there *is*, something slightly odd about me. At forty-five years old, it feels simultaneously liberating and terrifying to admit this. It is an oddness that has remained unnamed and undefined throughout my life. It is an oddness that has seen me assessed for a buffet of psychiatric disorders, all of which I can now see were symptoms of my undiagnosed oddness, rather than conditions in their own right. My chronic depression, my debilitating social anxiety, the diagnoses that flipped like landed fish – bipolar, borderline personality disorder, generalized anxiety disorder. I was always being told, *Well, it sounds a lot like . . .* and yet I was never able to fully solve the puzzle of myself and why I felt out of kilter.

At school my peers, even my teachers, could see the oddness in me. Bullies would sniff that oddness out. It was as if I was half out of frame in a movie, as if I, as a person, was never wholly in the picture. I recognized the oddness in myself as a very young child, or at least I recognized that my 'shyness' went further than shyness. It affected how I ate (chronic picky eater), the sounds I could cope with (fireworks terrified me) and the physical sensations I was comfortable with. I grew up by the sea but cannot stand the texture of sand on my skin. And though my family tried to teach me to change all of these things, tried to grow me out of the phase that I always seemed to be in (phases that have lasted forty-five years), I did not grow out of it. When I went to school, I was perceived by people who were not related to me. At school my oddness was more noticeable and worsened with the overwhelm of not quite fitting in. At school, struggling to make friends, or being close only to one or two people, I spent a great deal of time living in my own world, I spent a lot of time playing imaginative games on my own. I was never sure whether I was invited into the games that other children played, or what the rules were about asking to join. I have found throughout my life that there are unwritten rules about all social situations and while I can copy what other people do, I am missing some part of my brain that automatically knows what to do. It was only when I began school and saw myself reflected in the eyes of my peers that I recognized how the world saw me as strange, weird, odd. I was not *acting* oddly, I was acting like myself. And it was me that was odd to other people. I was not the norm.

At home, I could see some of this oddness mirrored in my family. It was in my dad's eccentricity, in my mum's shyness. But even at home I felt anxious, and I couldn't quite work out what was expected of me or how to integrate into the family. My anxiety was always there, and that was also a part of my oddness. I pushed away from myself, and I pushed away from the things that identified me as part of this tribe of oddness. In my teenage years, I wrote in my diary how much I hated myself, pages and pages of self-loathing and rules that I needed to follow to be liked, to be lovable and to fit in. To open those pages now feels like opening a wound, like sticking my fingers into a hot, angry pain that never quite went away.

When I first set out to write this book, I wanted to write about what it meant to belong to the landscape as a person from a rural working-class background. I wanted to write about what the landscape meant to me, because I'd seen so few of these stories written by people like me. However, as I began to write this book it soon became apparent that to discuss and explore the concept of belonging, I needed to recognize that there was a deeper sense of *not* belonging in me. I could easily identify the places where I had had to challenge assumptions and taboos around a sense of identity; they included being working class, infertile, bereaved, but many of my experiences of feeling out of place were being fed by another source, something that I found painful to admit to myself. I do not fit in. I am not like other people. To admit oddness is to admit that I am an outsider, and that is a vulnerable state to be in. But within that vulnerability lies a kind of strength. This, then, is a journey of interior landscapes as much as it is about exterior landscapes, because for me the two are intertwined.

Now, as an adult, I am awaiting an assessment for autism. Sometimes I think to myself, what if, after all this, you have the assessment and you are told no, this is not autism, you are as you always thought, just a person who cannot keep up, cannot fit in, that there is no underlying reason for this, no condition. Then I shall go on with my life unchanged, and I will accept that the parts of me that make me different are unchangeable. If I could have altered myself by hard work and determination, that change would have occurred by now. This self-examination, this long assessment of self and past, has not been without worth, because I now recognize that I do not need to change.

The only place I find a home for all my sensitivities and strangeness is in nature.

Years ago I thought that becoming a mother would be the answer, that I would pop myself back into the world like a dislocated kneecap being shunted back into place. I felt I would be able to fit in better with my sister, my mum, if we had shared experiences of motherhood, with my friends, but there was something else too. Motherhood seems so central to how women are perceived and accepted: as life givers, as something almost sacred. I wanted that connection, to be a link in a chain that stretched back to the beginning of time. But we found ourselves infertile and needed IVF to have a baby. More oddness, more not quite being right in the world. And then our daughter died, and the further IVF treatments ended in miscarriage or negative tests and then we stopped trying. The train that was a life with a family of our own carried on and away, and we found a different route. I lost the identity of mother.

When I thought of myself as working class that too carried a kind of shame. The class that I come from is always under pressure to conform to middle-class values and standards. To be working class is to be told to improve your accent, that you must aspire, that you must be socially mobile. To be rural working class is to be the butt of jokes about sheep shagging. To show yourself as happy to be working class is a strange thing indeed.

When I thought about my roots, it was to think about the pride that my dad had in his farming ancestry, that we had been farmers for generations, that his very name could connect back to generations of farmers before him. And though my dad was the break in that chain, though my dad was *not* a farmer, he saw himself embedded in it, and proud of it. I took that identity too, feeling a connection to a place I'd never lived, a life that I knew only through second-hand stories and a generational pride.

Over millennia, the lake site itself has transformed into so many different landscapes, it is many layered. I could see the ghosts of its past in the villages around its edges, and when the earth was peeled back by archaeologists, we saw a glimpse of what it had once been, its true form hidden under a skin of mud and rocks and grass. What *is* its true form? Before it was a lake it was a glacier, before the glaciers it was a different landscape, and before that it was a shallow sea. These were changes wrought by the natural cycles of evolution and creation. What we, as humans, had done to the lake was to change it, drain it, fence it, farm it, over hundreds of years we had forced it into a shape it never would have taken.

A part of my oddness is that I automatically assign human characteristics to animals, plants, even to inanimate objects. I become attached to them. I know I could never own a Henry Hoover because I would end up with a room full of them, never being able to take a broken hoover to the tip if it had a face on it. As a child, in the Co-op in Scarborough, I once poked holes in the boxes of a whole shelf of teddy bears because I worried the soft toys could not breathe. I created a complex system around choosing a stuffed toy to take with me to bed, fearing I would upset the others and leave them feeling left out and unloved. According to others, I was too soft and too sensitive. I had to harden up, get thicker skin. Something I never quite managed to do. Now, as I thought about how I might journey back to my authentic self, I questioned why treating animals, or even the landscape, with the respect one would treat humans with could be wrong. There were communities and religions that did just that, of course, and the Mesolithic Star Carr people had shown an obvious reverence for the animals that lived in this place and the landscape that provided for them.

I have always been attracted to rituals, to the displacement of emotion into a physical act, to the idea of pilgrimage as a practice in which the physical and the spiritual are merged. I have everyday rituals. My anxious brain relies on rituals to safely structure my life. I have a journalling routine that is a kind of ritual, and sometimes the act of being creative feels ritualistic. When I went out walking that too seemed to form a connection with a thing inside me that felt spiritual, natural. I'd left behind my Methodist church upbringing and had felt detached from religious and spiritual life for a long time, having previously drifted towards Buddhism, Quakerism, pantheism but never quite settling. Now I felt it was time to make my own landscape rituals, to find a way to acknowledge the magical, the reverent, alongside the practical landscape. I decided I would treat this ancient landscape, this ancient lake that I had driven around my whole life, as a place of reverence, rather than a backdrop. I would take a pilgrimage around the lake. I would make a series of deliberate journeys and consider my life in the context of this place. What if I could find a way to reconnect with myself by gaining a greater understanding and appreciation of the landscape I have always been embedded in?

There is a vague sense of ridiculousness as I sit in the layby and note in my journal all the things I want to do on this journey. I am giving reverence to an idea that seems, on the surface, unworthy of it. After all, I'm not about to climb Everest, or hike to Machu Picchu, or take a true pilgrimage to a holy place. I'm not taking a pilgrimage to an unknown place, or to a place of religious significance, but there *is* something spiritual about it.

There's a wind blowing across the valley that is fit to freeze the cheekbones. I drive over the land bridge in the blackness and catch the occasional bright eyes of sheep and cows reflected in my headlights. Then I'm back on the road ringing the lake, heading home to my own village and its tiny church with its distinctive corrugated iron roof and beautiful stained-glass depictions of jackdaws and swifts.

It is early March. The weather is beginning to feel more

like spring; the mornings and evenings are noticeably lighter. A rind of moon that has been visible for hours in the blue spring sky now becomes sharp and white as the sky deepens to violet. There is a lot of standing water in the fields. It is flinty and bright in the tractor tracks, and it pools and puddles in the valley where the water table is just under the surface of the land. We are emerging from a cold, wet winter. The temperature in the daytime has risen to a balmy eight degrees, and this morning I was able to sit in my conservatory with the door open and watch the jackdaws picking through the moss on the roof. I am longing for spring and the ensuing rush of life in the valley, though I am dreading the return of the overwhelming number of holidaymakers who will soon arrive at coastal towns; migrating to Airbnb cottages, holiday homes, caravans and campsites, returning to this place that they too may love, where they may well find belonging and a sense of peace. Some of them will return for good, escape to the country, retire and settle here forever. Some of them will buy second homes, their own roundhouses, to return to at will.

I return to my little ex-council house and the spare room that I call my office. It is a little haven of warmth and lamplight. I open the window to smell the breeze and hear the wind blowing the beech trees. I'm close enough to the coast to be able to hear the sea on nights when the weather is just right for it – it crashes against the rocks at the bottom of the cliffs and makes a booming sound, even when the air is quite still. A blackbird is singing its last song of the day from the top of the neighbour's garage. I sit in the dark listening to it, breathing in the smell of soil and grass, and am settled into a place of safety and stability, a sense of home that is embedded in this landscape. I make some more notes in my journal, list the things I want to accomplish, then cross them out, feeling self-conscious. It would be easier simply to continue untethered, I think, or at least not revisit myself like this. But I think of my dad again, and I think of my place in this world and how, at forty-five, I don't want to be distanced from the woman I am. I want to come home. I will return to the Palaeolithic lake site, the ghost lake that brims with my previous selves, and I will navigate its edges. I will thank it for my life, I will acknowledge it, know it. I will begin at the place where my wild self was reborn. I will begin at my daughter's grave.

# CHAPTER TWO

# Woodlands Cemetery

Each time I visit my daughter's grave, each time I drive up the tree-lined approach to the cemetery, I am taken back to the day of her burial. I am taken back to the pink blossoms drifting across the road. I am taken back to the way they settled in the hair and on the dark, sombre suits of the very few guests who were present, and the way that some of the petals went into the grave with her coffin.

When I look back, having emerged from the alternate world that is grief, I remember the way we fell into a series of rituals during her funeral, rituals that seemed almost choreographed, and I think how strange and beautiful the instinct behind that moment of grief was. After I had carried out her coffin, laid it on the ground on a green cloth, and the coffin was lowered into the grave, we formed a queue and each of us tore the rosebud heads off the flower displays and threw them onto the coffin lid. We took turns to do this thing, this rhythmic act of scattering petals. And then there was another line-up, one mixed with relief: a hug, commiserations, one after the other. There was a comfort in the rituals of that day, the soft flower heads, the sound of them hitting the coffin lid. They were our last chance to touch her, in a way. I imagine the rose-buds like a layer in a geological diagram: coffin, flowers, earth, grass, sky.

It's early June, early morning. I have the car windows down. I'm sitting in my usual parking spot, just outside the entrance to the children's section of Woodlands Cemetery. There is a slight breeze blowing up from the sea which lifts the smaller branches and leaves on the beech trees and hedges. It's a smooth shushing sound, like waves on the shore. It forms a pleasant sensory mirror to the blue line that is the sea on the horizon.

I have come here as part of my journey. This is the physical place at which things in my life began to change. While I was pregnant with my daughter, I could imagine being another person, something far away from the version of myself I was trying to escape, the woman who didn't fit in. I was going to be a mum. I was going to have a purpose – a good, clean, *wholesome* purpose – in the form of a beautiful daughter who would be with me forever. It is twelve years since I buried her.

The grief has worn itself down to something resembling a pebble in my pocket. In the beginning it was like a great sandstone block I couldn't carry, but now I run my thumb along the seam of grief, and it feels like an old friend – something familiar, something that is a part of me, something that changed me and made me.

The experience of loss, especially baby and child loss, changes people. The sheer force of that change is difficult to measure. I have been picked up and placed many miles away from the life that I had, and perhaps that figurative relocation has allowed me to see things differently. I feel I have a voice that I didn't have before. I have talked about grief a lot, even campaigned at Woodlands Cemetery to change the rules around leaving commemorative items on graves, trying to get the council to see the importance of this act for bereaved parents. I am not an expert on grief, but I am an expert on my own experience of grief, and in a world in which baby and child death is still such a taboo subject, a world in which we fear talking about death in general, I feel there is room for the bereaved to be listened to more.

I hadn't really thought about the ritual nature of my grave visits until Mother's Day 2018. I knew I was fulfilling a need in me, but if you'd asked me what that need was, I wouldn't have been able to tell you. It was only when I felt that my actions were being challenged and threatened that I lifted my head up from the grave and realized there was something else going on, something that wasn't just about tidying and making the grave look respectable.

I choose to use Mother's Day to remind myself that I *am* still a mother, even if the only child I've ever given birth to, the only child I ever *will* give birth to, died during that birth. On that particular Mother's Day in 2018, eight years after my daughter's death, I parked my car in the usual spot and saw, immediately, that something had changed. White laminated signs had appeared, dotting the peaceful landscape. The message on the signs was written in the same sort of tone that might be used on signs in the office tearoom, politely asking you to be considerate and wash up your own cups. Instead, they stated that the council wanted grave owners to remove all grave goods, except flower planters, leaving nothing that would impede maintenance or look messy. They were enforcing a rule that had been in the guidebook they gave me eight years before, when I was crawling over the rubble of my obliterated world and my thoughts were elsewhere. They'd assessed the graves. Someone had been to my daughter's grave and measured the size of the little fence we'd spent hours choosing. They'd assessed the little flowerpots and toys to see if they complied with the rules. Someone may have put their foot on the small plot of her grave and leaned over, nudging her things to one side to take measurements. They might as well have stood on her body.

Grief is a transcendental experience. I didn't recognize myself as an animal before my daughter's death. But I *am* an animal. The experience of this death has brought something more primal to the surface. And while I feel particularly protective about the grave site – instinctively, animalistically protective – this animal feeling has grown in me and grown out of me, into the life that I live away from this place.

I think we all have that wild in us, but perhaps we don't always know about it until it rises out of a wound. I am still surprised by it now, this animal that appeared in grief, demanding that its needs be met. It was so akin to the instincts of pregnancy, so like the cravings and nesting of pre-motherhood, like that of an orca, carrying the corpse of its dead calf for weeks at a time.

The laminated signs are still there, warning people not to messily grieve all over the graves of their children. I am still resentful. Even though I campaigned, petitioned, spoke on the radio, gave interviews and eventually got the protocols around the children's section of the cemetery changed due to the special nature of this sort of bereavement, the signs are still there. I can't help feeling that I have been patted on the head, I have been told what I wanted to hear.

Woodlands Cemetery opened in 1941. It must have seemed so modern and practical at the time. The people of Scarborough were used to the rambling Victorian Dean Road and Manor Road Cemetery with its enormous tombs, elaborate headstones and winding paths that curl off into secret areas and wind away beneath dank bridges. By contrast, Woodlands, set away from the centre of town and positioned with views out to sea, appears to have been designed to be practical and bright, embracing the scents of wood bark and the piney resin of conifers. A great deal of thought has been put into how the bereaved might wish to grieve privately.

When this cemetery was being laid out, a vision was being planted: of hedges the colour of burnished gold, set against the grassy hillside, the dark green of Row Brow Woods above, and the blue North Sea below. There is no rush here, no feeling of being watched. Each section has small entrances within the hedging, through which mourners might leave and enter without the awkwardness of having to step over neighbours who might be tending to a plot. A mourner could come to one of these enclosed spaces and sit by their loved one's grave and it would be intimate, personal.

In the original part of the cemetery, the feeling is one of being enclosed by nature, surrounded by trees and hedges. There are mature trees on the corners of each square, and the avenues between the grid layout are lux-uriously wide, allowing enough space for two cars to pass comfortably. The whole of the cemetery is lifted by the scent of the sea and the mulchy woodlands behind. The higher you climb up the slope, the better the view, until on reaching the top you can see over the rooftops of Scarborough town, over the local school, the hospital, and the spires of the many churches, to the castle on its promontory, the higgledy old town and further out to the white cliffs trailing away down the coast to Bempton, Flamborough, Bridlington and the wide North Sea.

At its highest point, the cemetery ends abruptly; the paths and roads and headstones butt up against Row Brow Woods, which continue as far as the eye can see. Row Brow Woods is part of a wider woodland complex, which joins Raincliffe Woods to the north and seeps down into the leafy, cool Forge Valley on the western side of the Tabular Hills – the flat-topped, table-shaped hills which edge the Vale of Pickering and the North York Moors. This ancient woodland is studded with Bronze Age burial mounds, several of which are right behind the cemetery. The effect of this woodland backdrop is that wherever you are in the cemetery, the sound of the forest ripples out. It is echoey. You can hear twigs snapping, animals passing through, and the sound of boughs moving in the breeze. It forms a soothing white noise. My daughter died with ventilators and resuscitation attempts, noise and sterility, and this place is the absolute opposite of that. I feel I have shushed her into the ground, here, truly put her at peace.

Today the air is cool with a sea fret, but already the June heat is burning the edges off that chill. The squirrels are making a ruckus in the branches above my head, and somewhere up near the woods something – a crow, a jackdaw? – is squawking. This is perhaps the thing I love the most about this place: the wildlife. There are squirrels, magpies, crows, sparrows and dunnocks. There are rabbits, foxes, and sometimes deer will come seeping out of the mist, making their way gently down between the head-stones, quietly clipping the grass. When I arrived this morning, a magpie was sitting on one of the headstones, its iridescent black and sharp white feathers perfectly suited to the rows of marble grave markers.

The road up to the top of the cemetery is steep and lined with headstones from the nineties. Some don't even have a name on, others have inscriptions that are almost letters to the dead, with every family member mentioned by name. The inscriptions on these headstones are keen to tell us that the person in the ground fell asleep, rather than died. Words are powerful. My daughter's headstone says she was 'born sleeping'. She wasn't. She died in between delivery and birth. There was a resuscitation attempt, a fight to bring her back, after we'd travelled from our local trust, whose care had been poor, to Leeds hospital, where she was born. Could I have coped with that language at the time? Perhaps the code that people use around death – the code of *passed away* and *born sleeping* – is about compassion for the bereaved, but some-times it is better just to say 'died'. On the day of her birth, her death, coming round from the light general anaesthetic, after the clamour of the emergency crash delivery, I asked for my daughter and a nurse told me she'd 'gone'. I had to get my husband to clarify whether she was alive or dead because 'gone' could have been a baby being whisked to ITU, or it could have been what it was, a baby in a cot, still warm, but not alive. Words have the power to carry trauma or relieve trauma. People find it difficult to be truthful when confronted with the need to deliver news which is so obviously going to cause immense pain to the receiver. For most people, it's in our nature to prevent pain. But I feel there is a genuine need for more guidance in the way that medical professionals in particular deal with the language around death. Being honest without being callous is a kindness, it allows people to begin, immediately, to deal with what has happened, rather than leaving them to work it out for themselves. Partly, though, I wonder how much of this is, again, my oddness that is at fault. I have found, especially in stressful situations, that I need information laid out in black and white in order for me to process it.

A squirrel arrives, moving up the line of headstones. I like seeing them here. They are emblematic of the living, the surviving, the nature that is benefiting from our place of death. This skinny wee thing looks like it has seen better days. I imagine it as a mother with a litter, run ragged trying to consume enough to feed her growing babies. She (let's call her she, though I have no idea how to differentiate male from female) stops to put her head into a flowerless flower holder, which must be filled with rainwater. She takes a good long drink. It confirms to me that putting a bird bath on my daughter's grave was a good idea, and I get a little thrill from imagining a squirrel drinking from it. It moves in the staccato way that squirrels do, hand-like paws occasionally rooting into the earth, presumably looking for last year's nut stash. And then it's gone.

As I get to the very top of the cemetery and walk along the road that crests the rise, the sound of the birds in the forest increases. A crow is rasping and there's a clumsy clatter as a wood pigeon breaks from the trees into the sunshine. I sit down on a bench overlooking the expanse of headstones and the Scarborough rooftops. It has a plaque on it, a donation from the Special Care Baby Unit at the hospital. I recognize it immediately as the bench I used to sit on when I would come to the cemetery daily to see my daughter. It must have been moved up here at some point and, yes, now I come to think of it, there is a bare spot of ground near the entrance to the children's section. How had I not noticed that before? Possibly it is because I no longer stay in the cemetery for any length of time when I visit. I have followed a drive, park, flowers, kiss, goodbye routine, but today has made a nice change. It has been a long time since I removed myself from the nitty gritty of grieving and looked about me.

The cemetery my daughter is buried in is the same cemetery where the sexual predator and Scarborough resident Jimmy Savile is buried. It is a fact that has consistently affected my peace of mind since he was brought here, to a spot in the cemetery, now unmarked.

I know where the grave is because I saw it in all its gaudy glory when he was first buried. At the time the grave was festooned with flowers and gifts, and people would come to gawp at the spot, which had to be fenced off with swags of metal rope. It had a huge black marble headstone in three parts – a tryptic of Jimmy portraits, Jimmy words and Jimmy celebrations. The whole thing was Savile's song of praise to himself: the charity work, the accomplishments, the poem about loving Scarborough which, as a poet, made me want to take a marker and edit it so the rhythm worked better. Even without the allegations that spilled out later, and the knowledge that went with them, it was uncomfortable to look at. Its lack of humility made me cringe. It dominated that section of the cemetery, and all the other headstones were dwarfed by it. In hindsight, the overbearing headstone looks like a deflection, or some sort of offsetting of good deeds against evil ones. I suspect that's exactly what it was.

My daughter was buried in 2010, and Savile was buried in 2011. 2011 was a tough year. But it was made tougher by the stream of tourists coming to see Savile's grave. One day, while I was kneeling next to my daughter's grave changing the flowers, a man barged in, right up to me, almost standing on the soft pink roses. Without any sort of preamble, he asked me where Savile's grave was. I was simmering with resentment and anger, but I felt obliged to tell him. It happened several times, but mostly people were more polite.

When he was exposed, after his death, as a serial sexual predator, the headstone was removed. The town was ashamed, and when people still came to see the spot, they took every identifier away. If you didn't know where to look, you'd miss the slightly discoloured grass, beneath which is concrete, protecting the grave itself from treasure hunters looking to rob it of its gold chains and medallions.

For the people left behind, external markers of loss are important. Even in cremation, when ashes are spread, they tend to be spread where the dead person had an emotional connection, and this place becomes the external marker for the people left behind. Of course, where cremation is concerned, this is a transient marker which only exists as long as the people who remember the spreading of the ashes are alive and able to share the memory of the place. When we mark a grave, it is for the people who are left behind. If grief is a continuity of the relationship one has with the deceased, then the markers that we use to define the place where a person is buried is like a halfway point – a letter to the dead, rather than a face-to-face conversation. It's more than that. It's a communication to the deceased, and a reminder to ourselves, but it's also a message to the community we exist in. It tells anyone who might be passing that this person existed, that they were cared about or at least they were thought of and remembered enough for someone to place something permanent, knowing that the physical form of a person is not. Long after the body is gone, the headstones remain. Remembrance of the true person – their personality, their traits and physical appearance – can only occur when someone still exists to remember them, but having the marker, whether it is a burial mound or a headstone, allows there to be a connection even without the living memory of the person who has died. How we remember the dead and having the space and facilities to carry out those rituals, no matter what shape they may take, are important.

Removing that external marker is a ritual in itself, a ritualistic striking out of the memory, but still, in a thousand years' time, when the headstones of this place are likely to be gone, the memories of the people lost, what will the people of the future infer from the graves themselves? There will be no tangible evidence of my daughter, and most of the people in the cemetery will be nothing more than darkened earth, but Savile – with his swags of indestructible gold, his chains and rings and belts – will appear to be a high-status individual, someone special. His wealth will give the impression of superiority and say nothing of his moral character. I think of the burial mounds of the lake people and their simple grave goods – pottery and flint, stones from the beach – and what they imply about their lives. I think of my dad in his wicker coffin, with just a crocheted blanket and a bed of hay, and my daughter, her small skeleton in a white coffin, a photograph, a letter from us and a stuffed toy.

The newest part of the cemetery is very basic. It is a field with a crop of headstones. There are no trees, no hedges, no fences. There are no magpies or doves or squirrels. There is just a blank of green, neatly aligned, and the mower has clearly been able to get straight across without hindrance. It has the feeling of being a storage facility for the dead.

I watch a small bumblebee clasping the head of a tiny blue flower which has somehow avoided being scythed down. Life finds a way. I walk past the rows of headstones back to the lower part of the cemetery and make my way to the area behind the toilet block. Here is a new development: a place for parents to bring the remains of their babies, babies who haven't made it to a point of any sort of certification of life. It is a gravelled area, with a purpose-built structure which looks a little like a spherical filing cabinet with small drawers. There's a bench at one end of the development, along with rows of small plots, and a container of planted flowers at the other. Each little plot has an identical granite flower holder. It is very neat, and yet the parents who have bought the plots to remember their babies have coloured outside the lines; there are toys and balloons, birthday cards and windmills spread all over the place, in the way that love, and grief, is untidy.

It's a perfectly acceptable place but there is no green, no grass. It feels not unlike a car park, and that makes me uneasy. I had a miscarriage in 2011 and another in 2012.

Around that point, visits to my daughter's grave became more structured and ritualistic. My grief manifested in my need to have something to 'do' at the grave. I planted things, I grew flowers, I enjoyed the sound of the trees above my head, the sound of birdsong, the bees and butterflies. There was a 'doing right by the dead' aspect and certainly a need to be parental, maternal, to care for the grave. I am also aware that it allowed me to connect to the ground and the soil, growth and death inextricably linked.

That sense of nature is missing in this gravelled area. It is as though we are afraid of the messiness and lack of control in nature, which is something that is reflected in our fear of death. We mostly die in hospitals these days. Our bodies are wheeled to mortuaries and from there to funeral homes and from there sealed in caskets and delivered into the ground or into the cremation chamber. It is almost as if death is an embarrassment, a failure of the ultimate goal of being healthy. When my daughter died, I had the opportunity to wash her body and dress her. I let the midwife carry out these simple acts while I watched, somehow afraid that I would break her, which is how all new parents must feel. Those moments we spent together and those few days on the ward with her body made a difference to my grief. They allowed me to process what was happening.

With my dad, we were able to sit with him before life support was turned off. We were there, comforting him as he died, though there was no way of knowing whether he could hear us. And afterwards we were able to have that last connection with his body. As with being with my daughter's body, that was an important part of the grieving process, the recognition that the body and the person I knew as my dad had separated – that he was gone.

With both the loss of my daughter and my dad, there were weeks when it felt like there had been a mistake, when I expected a phone call from the hospital to tell me there'd been a miracle, and my daughter had, after all, lived. Or that I would look up from the kitchen table at my mum's house and see my dad striding down the path with his battered old hat and oil-stained jacket. This too is a natural part of the grieving process as the brain reprogrammes itself to acknowledge the losses. Being around their dead bodies started that process. In nature, plants die, animals die, they decompose, and their bodies become the nutrients that other life needs to grow.

Nothing, then, ever really dies. The atoms are just reused in different combinations. This thought pleases me. It is reassuring in a way that religious ideas of heaven and the passage from one place to another never really were. My Methodist upbringing didn't feel like a structure I could cling to after the loss of my daughter, but nature did, landscape did.

This small, neat place of remembrance at Woodlands Cemetery is a perfectly adequate area, not unlike the gardens of many people (though not mine, mine is horrifically overgrown). But I find myself questioning how we can connect with the dirty, but ultimately natural, journey of death and grief if all we have as a place of connection is something hard, gravelly, scentless and silent? I wonder whether cemeteries could gear their design more towards supporting the grieving and less towards aesthetics and convenience. That might help ease parents' complex feelings around baby loss and child loss.

Surprisingly, I didn't mark my miscarriages in any way at all. Though I grieved for the two small lives we briefly created, there was not the same need to care for them, for myself. However, having spent some time in the infertility community supporting parents who have lost babies, I have seen lots of people do just this: take their baby's cherished remains home, at whatever stage they were lost, to bury in plant pots and gardens, planting trees and rose bushes on them, creating spaces to grieve, creating beautifully cared-for shrines. There is nothing growing in this place of neat lines and gravel. And that makes me sad.

I stand up and take a deep breath. The air smells faintly of seaweed, and the seagulls are wheeling above, the day sharpening with heat. I go to stand again at my daughter's grave. The little windmills are whizzing and the wind-chimes are clinking. I kiss my hand to the marble and tell her she is not forgotten.

# CHAPTER THREE

# Seamer Beacon

Seamer Beacon is a natural earth mound, covered in trees and surrounded by a Bronze Age burial ground. It is a visible marker, sitting proud on the horizon on the northern side of the lake site. If you know what you are looking for, the mound of Seamer Beacon is visible from almost anywhere in the valley. I am aware of it in my daily life, as I travel from my village into the nearby towns, as I drive along the edges of the long-gone lake, past the ghosts from my own life, my own past. I can see the mound while driving down the Vale of Pickering towards Malton and York, and from inland over the moors. It is such a prominent feature, rising on the lip of the valley, that it has become an emblem of home, a sign to look out for.

This whole valley – and the moors and the Dales and the Wolds too – is marked with signs of past lives and past deaths. It is a place of ritual and burial. The barrows and earthworks are meant to be seen, meant to connect the living to the dead, the present to the past. Barrows, also known as tumuli, are the burial grounds of prehistoric people. They are made up of earth and sometimes stones and are as individual as the communities who built them, people who used the local resources available to them. They are part of the umbrella term 'earthworks', which includes barrows as well as the raised banks and mounds associated with fortification. Earthworks are often all that is left to show us the activities of prehistoric people who lived thousands of years ago. It is a strange and beautiful coincidence that the mound itself, and the round barrows, are directly above the cemetery, *my* cemetery, the place where my daughter is buried. The ancient burial ground, my emblem of home, and the place I laid my daughter all those years ago are separated only by a semi-circle of ancient woodland: Row Brow Woods. This feels to me like a continuation of grief – something that connects us, me, to the ancient past.

It is July, a breezy, warm but overcast morning. I have come to Seamer Beacon to be close to the burial complex. Although I'm familiar with Seamer Beacon as a landmark, I have never visited the site up close. Now I want to see the burial mounds, climb the beacon, explore the liminal place where manmade structure becomes landscape, where the dead lake people meet me, a living lake person with my own dead, my own rituals and rites.

When I think about my experience of loss, I sometimes wonder whether the way that I reacted to grief, my daughter's death especially, was a case of me being 'too sensitive'. 'Too sensitive' was one of the labels given to me in childhood that I have attached a great deal of shame to. To be 'too sensitive' is to be too much, to be uncontrollably, animalistically, monstrously far away from 'normal'. To fit in, one must crush down the fear and hope and sadness and pain and not be the explosive thing that you are.

I grieved hard for my daughter, for years. There were people around me who could not understand that grief. After all, my daughter was pre-term, premature, might not have survived anyway, even if she had lived through the trauma of her birth. It is so easy to squash another person's experience like this. To discard her death as if she was a defective factory part sliding into a bin at the end of a conveyor line, rather than an actual person, *my* person. Later, after my dad died, I began to think about who will remember me after I have died. Although I have a niece and a nephew, with no children I have no one to maintain a grave, no one to carry my stories on down a chain, no one to recall my achievements, or my failures.

According to Historic England, Bronze Age barrows, and later barrows, are often placed near monument sites that have been used by earlier, Neolithic people. In fact, at the Seamer Beacon site, there is evidence of Neolithic occupation beneath the barrows. These burial mounds are not simply cemeteries, but monuments to the dead, they are made to be noticed, to be seen. I imagine that the Bronze Age cemetery was built around the prominent mound of Seamer Beacon because it was meant to be seen. The dead in the burial mounds were meant to be remembered by the people below in the village. Seamer Beacon would be a symbol and a tool of remembrance, the physical message in the landscape that told generation after generation that this was the place of their people, that even when the stories of the people buried there were long lost, the sense of belonging was not. I did this with my daughter, in a way, I placed a headstone over her grave with her name on it, and our names, and made a point of telling anyone passing that she was loved, that she was missed and remembered. When I am gone and can no longer carry her memory in me, can no longer write books about her or tell people about her, her headstone will still be there. My name too, will be on it. Perhaps that's enough.

I wish to acknowledge the effect the burial mounds have had on me, both as a sign of home, and as a reminder that grief has always been present, always happening to us, and that I am not alone. This will be my first pilgrimage to a place that I have no immediate connections to, a place that I have seen but never been in close contact with. This feels like the beginning of a journey. I will make my way up and above the cemetery where my daughter is buried and climb to the place where the Bronze Age community of lake people remembered their dead. I will make a deliberate, physical act of remembering them. I will travel to see the burial mounds, these memorials. I want to acknowledge their time spent here as significant, in the way that I want to mark the time my daughter spent with me as significant. I want to make sure these people are not just important in a historical sense, as a device for learning about ourselves and our own past, but as people living their lives, being ordinary, being important because they existed as human beings. I want to connect and acknowledge myself, my grief, and to forgive myself for being sensitive, for over-grieving. I hope that by seeing the monuments these people left, I can understand the sheer strength of grief. After all, grief is only the counterweight of love, and to love a child created in and born of your body is also to love yourself, to bury a part of yourself. There is nothing insignificant about that. There is nothing oversensitive about being in a state of grief that lasted many years, until we came to accept a life without her, without any children. Where is the sensitivity baseline over which one must never pass? Who sets the limits?

I want this pilgrimage to be spiritual. I am holding onto the idea of a pilgrimage as a devotional practice. I have been looking at the tonsure-like tumuli on my Ordnance Survey map, have walked my fingers over them obsessively, as if there is a puzzle to be solved between the contours and the dotted lines of bridleways and railway tracks.

I arrive at Throxenby Mere, just a couple of miles north of Scarborough, aiming to take the long route up the steep slope and through the ancient woods, a sort of diagonal approach to the top of the hill, where I can walk above Woodlands Cemetery, above my daughter's grave, and onwards to Seamer Beacon.

It's been thirteen years since I lost my daughter, and I find that I myself feel lost, even now, never wholly in one place or truly belonging. Walking in nature has always been a means of reconnecting with myself and my place in the world, and my walks are usually along the farm tracks around the village where I live, or occasionally on the high chalk paths of the Wolds. It's been a long while since I walked in a forest and immersed myself in the wild.

Today I want to make a pilgrimage through this ancient woodland to the Bronze Age burial site. I want to make a conscious effort to slow down, re-tune myself to the landscape, stop looking at it as merely the ground I traverse to get to where I am going and start seeing it as something other, something more meaningful. *I* want to feel meaningful.

There is a Japanese method of reconnecting to nature called *shinrin-yoku*, or 'forest bathing'. It's a superb name for what happens when one steps off the path and in among the trees. According to research by the German forester and scientist Peter Wohlleben, trees have their own communication systems and are aware of our presence, passing information through the fungal networks around their roots, alerting each other to the presence, or threat, of people. I am conscious of myself as an intruder among the trees and perhaps this is why I step so quietly, as if entering a church.

I tune in to my senses. The air feels damp, loamy. The smell of the reedy mere, the body of water I've just passed, is all around me, and the ground is puddled with black water. I am no more than ten feet into the trees when the sound, or lack of it, becomes a close, comforting thing. As I enter the terrarium of trees, the air becomes thicker, the ground becomes softer; I am walking over the life cycle of trees, the rotting leaves, the stuff of trees replacing their own nutrients through their roots. There is no birdsong and, for now, no animal movement among the trees. Time slows. I become slow too. I am bathing in the forest. It is like entering a lake; my surroundings become darker, the light, leafy edges of the woods are blotted out. I am submerged.

This place feels ancient in the way that the glacial valley feels ancient, and mountains feel ancient. There is a presence here. Even thinking such a thought makes me feel slightly embarrassed. I was a scientist in a previous life, before I was a writer, and am trained to see the facts in relation to action and reaction. But perhaps there is more to the world than facts laid out end to end.

In this part of the forest there are many patches of burned ground. There are illegal bonfire sites, the sharp scent of burned wood all around, and empty bottles and cans are strewn about, the detritus of the local teenagers. A man

with a dog is moving about the place with a delicate familiarity. He has a bin liner and a waste-collecting grasper
and he's clearing up after the night-revellers. We smile a
hello to each other and his dog, a silvery grey marbled
sheepdog, comes to greet me, gentle-eyed and soft-
muzzled, placing its head trustingly into my hand. I feel
a desire to help, a responsibility. I share a kindred concern
for this place, for keeping it clean and unstained. But today
I must continue on. The man picks steadily away, crab-like,
and I climb, digging my toes into the soft ground to steady
myself.

I see no one else for a while, though occasionally I hear
voices. In this dark part of the forest sound becomes
focused on the tread of boot, the steady step after step. It
really does feel like these tall, dark trees are watching me
weaving between them. And then, quite suddenly, I reach
an open chalk and brick road which stretches up the hill.
The forest continues on the opposite side, but I turn a hard
right, and step onto a steep path which is shored with
pieces of broken bricks, cement, cobbles and what looks
like rubbish – squashed bottles, bits of old metal, pen lids
and other everyday detritus – all crammed and wedged to
create a surer footing and, I imagine, drainage – some sort
of soakaway for what is still a very boggy path. It seems
strange to me that what appears to be landfill rubbish has
been used to do this, but I have seen, in the past, farmers
do the same thing, using rubble, broken crockery, broken
glass, etc., to create better drainage in areas of a field where
water pools, places where tractors need to get past. When
I see the rubbish from my own youth, I can't help but feel
that here is time becoming thin: the road packed with our
disposable waste, and the disposable waste is already
becoming history, wedged into the road to aid the passage

of future passers-by. I see cans and bottles from twenty years ago, recognize products from my childhood.

As I walk on, the road curves further up, becoming steep enough that I need to stop for breath. I've been moving steadily upwards until this point and hadn't realized that I have travelled sideways. It's heavy going. I have to keep stepping up onto the banks to avoid the thick mud, but the higher I go, the less groundwater there is, and it is a pleasure to feel my muscles pushing and pulling, to feel the rhythm, the force of grasping the branches of a living tree, using them to swing over puddles and uneven ground.

Everything on this part of the journey is magnified. I am paying attention not to the surroundings, not to the wider scope of the valley, but to where my foot is, where my hand is, how I grasp, how I push forward. The world becomes small enough to notice individual leaves, the roots of trees, the flower heads and insects, because climbing and grasping and forcing my body up through the woods is causing me to be eye level with it, literally, in places. There is something mindful about it, being so present, and I'm reminded of doctors who prescribe outdoor activities to heal trauma.

During my transition from scientist to writer, at a point in my life when I needed not to be reliant on training or specific skills and needed only an ability to walk in nature, I worked as a dog walker. The work was often miserable. I discovered that many, many dogs do not like to walk in the rain, in the heat or with strangers. I learned that people expect an awful lot from you for eight pounds an hour if they think you're an unskilled worker. But I also learned how to physically slow down. How not to rush. If a dog refuses to walk, you cannot force it, you must stop. I spent a great deal of time standing under trees avoiding heavy showers. In fact, my abiding memory of that part of my own journey is of standing beneath dense foliage in silence, with a dog at my side, both of us motionless, listening to the sound of the rain on the leaves and watching the puddles ripple.

I stop to catch my breath and look up towards the rim of the slope. I am conscious of the round barrows above me, just out of sight, and that the landscape I am traversing hasn't really changed a great deal since the builders of these mounds were here, possibly walking this route, pulling themselves up through the trees, their voices echoing through the forest.

The barrows are much more complicated than they appear, the structures must have taken some time to create, and must have involved much lugging of materials from around the area. I think about what these workers did when it rained. Did they shelter under the trees of Row Brow Woods, listening to the patter on the leaves? I feel most connected to this area, and the people who came before me, when I think about people doing ordinary things. Not when I think about great and wonderful graves like Sutton Hoo, but these places of respect and remembrance for regular people, the non-elite. That a person might have paused here and placed their hand, like I have, on the smooth bark of a sycamore and stood, leaning into the shelter, waiting for the storm to pass. It creates a sense of connection much deeper than when I gaze at the gold and jewels of ancient peoples, stuff that sits behind glass in London museums.

As I move between the trees and the path, searching for the surest footing, I realize that I am by far the noisiest animal in the woods. It pleases me that I am, at least, certainly an animal now, no longer the padded stuffed armchair of the human state. I can feel myself opening, becoming watchful. My ears have tuned in to every cracked twig and moving leaf. I feel, as I always do when out in the landscape, that I am living rather than just existing. The ground around the trees is much greener here, with ferns and bracken and so many wild foxgloves and honey-suckles I begin to think that there may have been some guerrilla gardening going on. There are bees and flies and midges and finches, everything is alive with movement and colour, and as I turn to walk along a ridgeline, I can look down where swathes of trees have been felled for farmland. I can see that I have almost reached Woodlands Cemetery, am almost rising above it, can almost see my daughter's grave, but not quite. Then the road rises again, and I am climbing away, and now the wide track narrows to a single track, a true hollow way, with curved sides and foot-polished rocks, edged in sandy soil. The roots of trees drape onto the path, the canopy above me forms a tunnel, leading me onwards.

There is a piece of rock poking out of the soil, and when I prise it out I see that there is a fossil in it. I can't tell what kind – maybe a coral or a fern, maybe an eroded ammonite. It feels like a sign. It reminds me of the Gryphaea I found in the field where I walk my dog, the field from which I can see Seamer Beacon, the hill I am journeying towards today. That day I was looking for a sign, anything that would give me reason to believe the IVF – our one and only NHS go at IVF – would work. The anxiety was eating at me, and I was searching for meaning in magpies and signs in the ground. And there it was, a huge curl of a thing, a 'devil's toenail', which fitted perfectly into my palm like an enormous sleeping wood-louse. It was the biggest, most perfect specimen I'd ever found. It has sat on my desk ever since. When I look at it, I can still see myself holding it up, on the day I found it, examining it in the sunlight, just like I am holding this fossil up to the light now. Both times I have been facing the beacon and the burial mounds, only this time I am so much closer, and my daughter is below me and time has sluiced through the middle of it all.

I duck under a fallen tree, an archway between the woods and the farmland beyond, a mossy portal through which I must pass to reach the summit and then, like a cork popping out of a bottle, I am out and at the top of the hill, suddenly above the valley and beneath a wide blue sky. The air around me is full of birdsong and the sound of the breeze in the fields. In my path are several enormous mobile phone towers; their steel buzz is unnerving, and the generator shed behind is surrounded by padlocked fences, razor wire and signs threatening death by electrocution. It's a shock to wash up next to something so manmade, so deadly.

Almost immediately there is a barrow to my right, but it is behind a barbed wire fence, with no admittance. It's the first one I've seen up close and, in my excitement, I mistake it for Hagworm Hill, the wonderfully evocative name of one of the barrows I've seen on my OS map, 'hagworm' being a colloquial name for the adder, a reasonably common snake round these parts.

Later I will find out that Hagworm Hill was excavated and deconstructed years ago, on behalf of the Department of Agriculture, to enable easier ploughing for the farmer. It is still a registered monument, but that monument is unseen, a ring of kerb stones, a crop mark that can only be observed from the air.

Something about this first barrow says *manmade*, but

I'm not sure why. The barrow is an island raised above the meadow. It has a shape that suggests constriction, as if a band has been placed around its middle and squeezed tight, forcing the earth to spill up over the rim. There are rowan trees and a small oak on its top.

The breeze blows at my back as I cross the ploughed field, sticking to the thick ruff of grass and thistles on the verge. I see a gate with a public footpath sign, and a warning of escaped cows if the gate isn't shut, and as I turn the corner, there it is, the journey marker I've been searching for: Seamer Beacon.

It is unbelievably peaceful, the field thick with finches, sparrows, blackbirds, even a woodpecker somewhere, and not at all as I expected. I thought it would have the sombre feel of a graveyard, but it doesn't at all. It is a soundscape, a scent-scape, a place where I can imagine bringing a book and sitting for the day. Someone has been here before me; a trail of footprints leads through the dew-wet grasses to the base of the hill. They must have been here very early, and now there is no one else here but me.

The land that the burial complex and Seamer Beacon sit on was once owned by Albert Denison Conyngham (1805–1860), also known as Lord Albert Conyngham and Baron Londesborough. Albert Denison was president of the British Archaeological Association. He was a keen amateur archaeologist but, like many gentlemen antiquarians of the time, his scattergun approach may have caused more damage and confusion, rather than the expansion of knowledge for those following in his footsteps. It certainly made it difficult for me, a non-archaeologist, to work out where the barrows were and who had excavated them. I want to know the story of this manmade landscape – what is original, what is ploughed out, what still perseveres thousands of years since it was created – so it is important to me to work out the timeline of the place and who had a hand in its reshaping.

Even with a combination of excavation reports from the 1970s, Ordnance Survey maps, Google Earth and older maps from the nineteenth century, the timeline is still confusing. Although the barrows are described as 'interesting' in the 1970s archaeological reports, these are not significant barrows, and so finding information about them is a challenge. These barrows do not contain the sort of grave goods associated with the elite. They are the burial places of people who lived and farmed this area, the families and chieftains of the tribes who chopped down the forests and planted crops – people who might, at a stretch, fit into our modern idea of 'working class'. These barrows are unlikely to add an awful lot more to our knowledge of the migration of the people who brought metalworking or farming practices to Britain. There is no gold buried within them, no world-shattering discoveries. They are just the markers of people passing through this life, living in the valley.

A ceremonial cup, or lamp, was discovered here in one of the excavations. This small, stone object, with a hollow centre and perforated sides, decorated with incised lines, was likely used either as part of a funerary ritual, or as a lamp to light dark rooms. It featured in the wonderful 2022 British Museum exhibition 'The World of Stonehenge'. In fact, it was the first object to greet visitors as they entered the low lights and hushed sound of the exhibition space. The ceremonial cup is kept in the local museum by Scarborough Museums Trust and was loaned to the British Museum because of its connections to Stonehenge: the markings and perforations around the edges give the appearance of the Stonehenge monument itself, and there was a similar cup found in the grave of a 'woman of high status' near Stonehenge. But whereas the Stonehenge burial contained gold items, items which have been displayed in the British Museum and at the Stonehenge Visitor Centre, the Ayton Moor burial, where the ceremonial cup was discovered, contained only flints, bone and stone, items that stayed within the local museum's archives.

In the excavation reports written by Albert Denison in the *Journal of the British Archaeological Association*, he writes about his excavations of several other mounds around Seamer Beacon, on Irton Moor. The reports give an impression of someone treasure-seeking: digging a hole in a mound, turfing out the bones and teeth of the dead, collecting the sherds and food vessels, then moving on to the next. Archaeological practices have changed since Denison's time, but I can't help but feel annoyance at this slapdash approach. He was, at least, someone with an interest and a passion and it pleases me that many of the urns, vessels, flints and remains are now protected and archived in the British Museum. That said, the British Museum is very far away from this little place on a moor in North Yorkshire. I cannot simply go and visit. It is outside the limits of my budget, outside the limits of most local people's budgets. It would be an expensive expedition to go to London to see the things the lake people left behind here.

Albert Denison was the creator of a folly, built on the top of Seamer Beacon. It takes his name, Baron Albert's Tower, and is no more than a circular foundation of stone with the name carved into a block of sandstone. The point of the folly is to look like the ruins of something from an earlier age. I wonder why he chose to place this folly here, where there were so many areas of prehistoric value. I climb carefully over the folly, to the highest point on Seamer Beacon, and turn slowly, taking in the view from every direction. The wind is free up here. The two closest tumuli are so close that one of them is touching the hill of Seamer Beacon, nestled against it like a lamb to a ewe. There are marbled cows in the field to the north and to the west another tumulus, and another. Three tumuli next to the Seamer Beacon. This is a cemetery complex. Originally there were six or seven barrows near Seamer Beacon, and an extensive, extended complex of around seventeen barrows across the three moors of Irton, Ayton and Seamer.

I try to imagine the landscape as it was when the burials were taking place. The weather would have been about the same, a bit warmer perhaps. There would still be quite a lot of boulders, grit and gravel on the ground, left over from the receding glaciers, and more woodland, more trees at higher levels. I begin mentally removing the landscape around me, like a child packing a farm set away in its box: perhaps no hedges, no boundaries, as early Bronze Age people seem to have been quite nomadic in their farming practices, moving their animals around the landscape. No fields of crops, or at least no blanket corn or wheat or barley – no pesticides or herbicides, so perhaps more birds then, more insects? No imported animals so no rabbits, no grey squirrels. The ghost lake would not be a ghost. It would be a swathe of water in the valley bottom. The water would be visible from the burial mounds. It must have looked like a silver slit in the earth.

The 1970s archaeological reports suggest that some of the barrows are aligned to the winter solstice. The shape of the stones that formed the internal structure of the barrows gave an indication of an 'entranceway' into the barrow. This entranceway – seemingly ceremonially blocked by a large rock when the barrow was closed by the people who built it – was aligned to the point at which the sun would rise over the lip of the valley on the shortest days of the year, around the 21st December. Usually I spend the solstice at home, in my office. I have made a mark on the wall where the sun hits it at the solstice sunrise. I like the ritual of beginning, of watching through the trees outside my window as the sun creeps across, silently turning the year from dark to light. I make a mental note to come back one day, for the solstice sunrise, to be present with the lake people as the sun crawls over the valley. There would be clearer skies, less cloud cover. But it would be the same horizon, the same sea, the same sun. Despite this knowledge, it is still difficult to imagine their world. I find a more human connection in the grave goods, what grave goods there are. The pottery urns or food vessels found in most of the barrows in this complex are of a fine, skilled workmanship, and more, they bear a striking resemblance to pottery found in other barrows up and down the Vale of Pickering and out into East Yorkshire and the Yorkshire Wolds. There is a theory that one or two skilled potters made them all. I imagine this potter who travels nomadically between settlements, bringing his pots. Perhaps *he* is a *she*. Perhaps they bring the clay with them, and make their pots to order, perhaps there is a family of potters, a thriving business. They eat well. They make good pots. Perhaps one of these graves is their family mound. In one sherd from the Barrow III excavation there are fingernail imprints. I would like to find that piece of pottery and place my fingernail into that groove and know this potter's hands. I think about how precious these pots must have been. The families may have given up their best belongings to the dead, in the same way, perhaps, as we fork out for fancy coffins for our own. I think about the famous Neolithic village of Skara Brae, in Scotland, and the stone dressers in the stone houses, where archaeologists believe the inhabitants' best pots were displayed, straight opposite the doorway, for any visitor to the home to see. I think about the lake people and their belongings, these people and their lives around this lake, the way they moved and walked and carried and hoisted and farmed and lived here and left nothing of their lives, only their deaths, marked on the horizon like messages. In Barrow III there were 'water-worn quartz stones' among those laid in the cairn. They must have gathered these from the nearby beaches. They must have gathered these shiny, pretty stones from the beach, stones which probably had other meanings, in the way that we have always ascribed symbolism to things we like or dislike. Some of the barrows are situated over 'pits', deliberately dug spaces, maybe fire pits or hearths, which predate the burial mounds. Some of the barrows contained Neolithic objects. The Bronze Age people must have looked back at the Neolithic people in the same way that we look back at Roman Britain, or the Middle Ages. Perhaps they had precious relics to pass along from an earlier age. This sense of needing some sort of chain of connection resonates with me. It's what I am doing, searching for myself in these places. My research tells me the Bronze Age people continued to use the stone circles and ritual centres of this earlier age, adapting them to their needs, and that the barrows themselves were often long-term projects, being adapted and added to with burials and cremations at later stages until one day they were no longer in use and gradually the people and their lives and their beliefs faded away.

I make another slow turn, noting the landscape and its raised points: Scarborough Castle, Jacob's Mount, the valley, the cliffs, Ravenscar, the moors. It's likely that the people whose cemetery this was lived nearby. It's possible that one of the villages I can see on the banks of the ghost lake grew from these people's settlements. And now here I am, rippling up to the edges of the barrows, lapping up to the graves, looking for roots, for connection.

It is time to leave and return to my own village. As I reach the bottom of the mound and turn to walk across the meadow, a quartz in the sandy earth catches my eye. It is smooth, caramel-coloured, with sparkling crystals running through it. Pilgrim badges – tokens to remember a pilgrimage by – have always been popular. I put the little stone in my pocket, along with the fossil I found earlier. These are my first pilgrim badges. I take them home to sit on my desk with the Gryphaea.

# CHAPTER FOUR

# Star Carr

It is September. My mum and I are walking across farmland, around the edge of the ghost lake, heading to Star Carr and the Mesolithic hunting site there. We are distracting ourselves from the heavy work of grief. I watch her small frame, even smaller since my dad died, moving through the landscape like a wading bird moving along the edge of a vast body of water.

This visit to the Star Carr site marks the first time I've been here since I was a teenager, riding on the back of my brother's scrappy trail motorbike, whizzing along the lanes and farm tracks, helmetless, with wild abandon. I can see myself so clearly, the chalk dust spooling behind the bike, pigeons scattering into flight, farmers stopping their work to see what the commotion is. And over that image, here I am, placing my feet in the same places, plodding on that chalk road, thoughtful and calm. I'm glad that writing this book has brought me back. I'm glad that I get to be here as the person I am now, remembering my teenage self, reaching out to her with compassion. There are other versions of myself here too – they flutter in my peripheral vision as I walk. I am picking my way through all these memories, all at once. Different versions of myself are layered in this place, like geological strata.

I wanted to bring my mum here to tune in to her own memories of the Star Carr site. She's lived within walking distance for fifty years. It is from my mum that I get my own head-down walk, my habit of scanning the ground for nice stones, fossils, interesting feathers. It was my mum who accompanied me on school trips to archaeological digs. Sometimes I wonder where those interests might have taken her, what she might have been, had she not married and had children. Sometimes I think she does too. She likes to research her family tree, likes to know the history of the place she lives. She did well in geography, maths and English at school. As a teenager she went to secretarial night school so that she could better herself, do well, and get a job where she could use her brain more than her hands.

Our relationship is one of shared interests. We're not exactly close, but we're certainly not distanced either. We don't do very many mother–daughter activities, or rather we didn't. But now my dad is dead we find ourselves drifting up against each other. He was buried six weeks ago. We are still adjusting to his sudden death. My mum still says *we* and *us* and *our* – her brain hasn't caught up yet. When we talk about her car needing new tyres, she says, *Your dad says they're all right for a bit yet . . .* and it is like he has chosen to communicate details of car maintenance from beyond the grave. But it is not that at all. To my mum, frozen in loss, that conversation has happened minutes ago, one of those completely normal and irrelevant conversations that has suddenly, because of its proximity to the loss, become relevant, precious even. She is not yet ready to let that go. There will come a time when the year will have folded round on itself, overlapped these mundane marriage conversations, and he will no longer be present in this way. We will no longer be able to call on his last scraps of knowledge. He is already beginning to fade away from the house my parents shared.

My parents' house is now *not* my parents' house; it is my mum's house. His shirts are no longer in the washing basket, but his coat and hat remain on the chair by the back door. Parts of my own brain have adapted to his death, but still I find myself thinking, while preparing to have a new kitchen fitted, *I'll see if Dad'll help me rip the old cabinets out.* He is there in my mind: dirty jeans, knitted blue hat, oily coat, calloused hands. He is putting his toolbox down, not waiting to be invited to begin, pulling at the worksurfaces as I run to catch up and help. And then he's gone again. I remember that he's not here, and I can't ask him to help me do this. I can't ask him anything anymore. There's a sharp pain that unspools into a dull ache when I think of all the things I'll never talk to him about, all the stuff he'd have found interesting in this book, all the things I wanted to ask him about his own family, his own connection to the land.

As we pass the hedgerows, we point out all the different plants. Hawthorn, elder, brambles, crab apples. Walking past a hedge full of rosehips, my mum tells me how, as children, she and her siblings were paid by the council to pick rosehips to be made into rosehip syrup. It was extra income for a family with very little. She says, *They gave the syrup to the council house kids, the poor kids, so they didn't get scurvy.* This was post-war Britain when access to citrus fruits from abroad was limited. My mum was also one of the council house kids who got the syrup. She benefited two-fold. I can't imagine this happening anymore; not poor kids being given help with nutrition, but that the council, the government, would utilize plants growing in hedgerows, like a kind of hunter-gathering. When I was little, my mum used to treat our coughs and colds by making tea with leaves from a plant called colts-foot that we foraged around the railway tracks. I've read in the RSPB pocket nature book that the plant is called 'coltsfoot' because the leaves resemble a horse's hoof. But as a child I was always told that it's because the stem, when broken open, is U-shaped, like the sole of a hoof. Dried and steeped, then loaded with honey, it was not a bad drink.

Today we are visiting a place of true hunter-gatherers. Star Carr is a Mesolithic habitation site, dating to around 9000 BC. It's a place where, archaeology has shown, people visited the site for hundreds of years during the middle of the Stone Age. The Mesolithic period came after the Palaeolithic and before the Neolithic. Palaeolithic is the Old Stone Age, Mesolithic is the Middle Stone Age, and Neolithic is the New Stone Age. When I think of Palaeolithic people, I think of cave dwelling people learning to use fire, painting their hands on the walls of their caves, learning how to be human. The Mesolithic people existed after those cave dwelling people, but before the Neolithic people, people who learned to farm rather than forage, who built settlements and were no longer nomadic. The Mesolithic era has always seemed to me like a liminal period – a time when people passed from being animal-like in nature to seeming very human.

It's difficult to say what the exact purpose of Star Carr was, but it appears to have been the site of special rituals.

It's such a long time ago that, even with a wealth of well-preserved discoveries recovered from the peat, we are still reliant on interpretation based on what we 'think' was happening here. And this interpretation is through the eyes of people very, very far removed from the lives of the Star Carr people, so far removed that it is almost impossible to understand the significance of some of the finds. Interpretation is so easily influenced by modern-day perceptions that in order to avoid accidental bias research has to be quite rigid. There needs to be a balancing act between avoiding seeing oneself reflected in these people and therefore interpreting their actions and reactions based on our perceptions, which are influenced by a twenty-first-century mindset, and finding ways to humanize the people living so many thousands of years ago in order to use the experience of being human to interpret their actions. Although I'd like to know the lake people intimately, would like to know their culture, I also like the idea of them not giving up the secrets of their lives to us. Some things should perhaps be held sacred. If we know the truth in everything, we lose the magic from it too, and Star Carr *is* magical, a mystery.

For a long time, the Mesolithic period was defined only by the two periods that bookend it. These days it has attained more significance, and the Star Carr site is possibly the most important reason why. The discoveries at this site showed that the Mesolithic people were living complex, advanced, cultural lives here. No longer the loincloth-clad, spear-wielding, grunting people of past Stone Age perception, these Middle Stone Age people have been brought to life by years of work by archaeologists. Those archaeologists have diligently peeled back the layers and revealed the Mesolithic people's highly skilled tool building, their ritualistic behaviours, the warmth of their hearths. This is where they have come to life.

As we cross out of the country lanes, the land opens to us. The fields we are passing are potato fields. They supply the McCain's chip factory. The soundscape here is one of distant industrial alarms, reversing lorries and the rumble of tractors. It is overlaid with the sound of rustling grasses and reeds, the call of geese, ducks, skylarks. We watch a tractor with a trailer loaded with freshly harvested potatoes delicately crossing a tiny bridge over one of the many drainage dykes. Its slow rumbling and enormous wheels are strangely thrilling up close. We flatten ourselves to the hedge as it turns, reverses a little, turns again, then rumbles away at some speed up the chalk lane.

In the time when I was at school, my mum worked as a secretary for the big potato farm, and sometimes as an office cleaner there. These were typical farm offices – Portakabins and converted barns, usually with a small team of women to file and write letters, and a farm manager who would come in and out, the workers reporting to pick up their wage packets on a Friday. I have a sudden memory of meeting her after school in one of the offices, a portable heater at her feet, her small white hands typing diligently at an old-fashioned electric typewriter.

The farmers round here call this place 'the black lands', and the soil really is black. Black as the night. The ground is rich with fossils, and there are fossilized scallop shells that are so pristine they look like they might have been alive ten minutes ago. The shells come from a time when the whole of this area was under a shallow sea, a hundred million years ago, long before the lake, long before the valley, long before people. The shells glow like stars in the black soil. I pick up three in quick succession. They are rough on the surface but when I touch the inside they are smooth and pearlescent. The scallop shell has been a symbol of pilgrimage for centuries, the lines radiating out of the shell representing the many paths to a pilgrim site. These three shells, then, will be added to my pilgrim badge collection.

The small wooden bridge that we need to cross to get to Star Carr has been broken for months, the land impassable, but on this day a bunch of chatty council volunteers are working to fix it. They ask where we're going, and we talk to them a little about their volunteer work. They are joyous, savouring the company and the outdoors. When I ask what they get out of their work with North Yorkshire Council, they tell me it is about being proud of your environment, ensuring everyone can access it and experience it.

How we interact with nature is individual, and people approach nature in different ways. For me it is sensory. I think about this as I trip-trap over the little bridge, enjoying the sound of my boots on the fresh pine surface. I ask them if they know of Star Carr, and they do, or at least they know the importance of it, and they've heard of the 'oldest house in Britain'. This is the house that we are seeking out today. It's not really a house, it's the ghost of a dwelling place. But it's one of those images that catches the imagination. People live in houses now. People lived in houses then. You would not recognize it as a house if you saw it – it is not like a bungalow in the suburbs – but it is the concept of this house that makes it exciting. It is a place that was returned to, a permanent structure for people who had previously seemed to be completely nomadic. When I think of the houses I have lived in, I can list eleven, but only two of them have felt like home: the house I grew up in and the house I live in now. Both homes are at either end of the lake.

We move across the field on a public footpath, passing the place that is marked 'ancient settlement' on the OS map. The voices of the volunteers fade away. We are gently shifting sheep out of our way, trying not to frighten them. The ground feels vaguely spongy in places. The house is something only an archaeologist could detect – a dip, a slight discoloration to the soil. When they discovered it, the archaeologists saw the remains of a structure, several structures in fact, something that might have been tepee-like or domed, hide-covered or reed-covered, with the ground scattered with flint and the indications of a reed flooring.

The Star Carr site was in use for around eight hundred years. What is the modern-day equivalent of a house like the one found at Star Carr, where successive generations of people returned over hundreds of years to the same place, maintaining it and using it for the same purpose? I'm thinking about how we use religious places like churches, how we maintain them not just as buildings, but as sacred spaces within which spiritual acts are carried out. There were fewer people on earth in the Mesolithic era, so much less structure of society, so there was little to get in the way of a connection to nature. Whereas we, in the twenty-first century, are trying to commune with nature through a wall of built-up societal expectations and norms. We have to seek out nature to experience it. We commune with nature over a distance. Our norm is no longer to be a part of the natural world but to observe it. I imagine this place, these structures, as being something so much closer to the elemental, and what it means to survive on the senses, what it means to be within nature, rather than observing

it. I don't suppose we'll ever really know what these enigmatic people felt about their lives, their landscape. We have
only shadows of post holes and circles of flint flakes to
interpret their lives.

Star Carr is secretive, and it exists within the imagination
as much as in a physical location. Mum and I are struggling
to find the site, never mind the house. It's difficult to see
which field it is in. There are electrified fences along the
redirected river. The place is much less wild than I
remember, much neater. It has been contained. We walk
up and down the ditches, unaware that we keep walking
past the site, keep walking over some of it.

As we walk, my mum talks about the visit we made in
the eighties to a site up the road, a school trip to Heslerton
and an Anglo-Saxon or Early Medieval burial ground. I
have a patchy recollection of it: orange bus seats with that
spiky material that left patterns on the backs of bare legs.
A day turned rainy, an invitation to sit in the Heslerton
village school and eat our sandwiches. She remembers it
better than me. She says the famous archaeologist Dominic
Powlesland was there, that we, or she, talked to him. That
he was enthusiastic, that he enthused us. Later, when I talk
to Nicky Milner, the archaeologist who has, perhaps, done
the most to bring the Mesolithic out of the dark, she'll tell
me that she was a sixteen-year-old archaeologist at that
same site, and I'll wonder if our paths crossed, if she was
part of the delicate web of events that led me here, to this
point, today.

My mum also came to see the Star Carr site back in the
eighties when it was being unpeeled from the ground. She
describes the scene: the long deep trenches, limber archaeologists crouched and kneeling. It looks so different now.
It is, after all, hidden, buried. The land we are standing on

is working land. It is part of the history of the valley, and it also serves a modern-day function. The A64 rumbles past, the sound of farming and industry drifts over the fields. To the north is the village of Seamer and the Seamer Carr Household Waste and Recycling Centre, and the huge landfill dump, the methane vents like toy windmills catching the sunshine. To stand on the Mesolithic site of Star Carr is to stand in a field, not far from a busy road and with an enormous rubbish tip in the background. You need to have a good imagination to visit the site and be awed by its significance.

John Moore discovered the Star Carr site in the summer of 1947. It was a summer of thunderstorms and burning heat. The valley was tinder dry around the edges, but in the bowl of the valley the carrland held water still, as it had for millennia. Moore was a local amateur archaeologist, and one of the founding members of the recently created Scarborough Archaeological and Historical Society. The members of the society were looking for a place to begin their excavations. They had split up and each taken a section of the local countryside to examine for potential archaeological interest. Moore had decided to look at the Vale of Pickering, specifically the area to the east of the vale, around the farming villages of Seamer, Flixton and Folkton. It is an area which he suspected might once have been a lake. This is a landscape he knew well. He knew the walls of the valley were carved by glacial activity. He knew how the mist rose over the carrs and how, in places, the ground rippled like water beneath one's feet. He knew how to navigate the fences, how to find paths around the ditches and diverted river. He was walking the marshy fields when he made his discovery.

As he crossed the area the local people called Star Carr,

Moore happened to look into the water channel that was the diverted River Hertford and saw, about five feet down, poking out from the striations of gravel, the point of a worked flint. I can imagine the sun catching the chipped edges, the way it glittered in the light. I imagine him clambering down the side of the ditch, pulling out the flint and seeing more – a piece of antler, another worked flint. I imagine this moment like a match about to be lit, a moment when light was about to be cast down the long tunnel of time, a moment in which he doesn't know, yet, that he has just discovered arguably the most important Mesolithic site in Europe.

Moore's story peters out a little after this point. He dug some experimental trenches to confirm the presence of prehistoric artefacts and then, on the advice of the local museum, he contacted Dr Grahame Clark, an archaeologist at Cambridge University. Grahame Clark had a keen interest in the Mesolithic period, and he had been looking for a waterlogged Mesolithic site where organic matter might be preserved. He knew there were sites like this in Europe and was keen to make his name and find one in Britain. Clark wasted no time in coming to visit the valley, recognizing that what had been discovered could aid our understanding of the people who came to make their home here over eleven thousand years ago.

Moore relinquished control of the site and gave Clark permission to dig Star Carr while he concentrated on another area nearby, Flixton Island, where he had discovered Palaeolithic tools and ancient horse bones. Moore becomes a footnote in the story of Star Carr from here on. There are some archived letters between him and the museum, but not much else. The letters are mainly regarding funding applications and records of museum acquisitions. Moore offered his own field notes on Star Carr and the Flixton lake area, but the museum declined, and now these notes, it seems, are lost to history.

In the time of Paleolake Flixton, the Star Carr site would have been a small promontory of land jutting into the lake. Occupation of the site began right at the start of the Mesolithic period, around eleven and a half thousand years ago. People arrived here less than one thousand years after the glaciers had receded. In those thousand or so years the land was left to itself. In the wake of the glacier, grasses, woodlands and reeds emerged. Into the woodlands came animals. Ducks, geese, roe deer, red deer, elk, wild cats, wolves, pine martins. I imagine an ecosystem ticking along: the predators and the prey, the seasons passing with no humans to acknowledge or record them. *If a tree falls in a forest and nobody is there to hear it, does it make a sound?* In this pre-people place, everything is connected – the ants eat the fallen fruit, the birds eat the ants, the pine martins eat the birds, the wolves eat the pine martins. Everything is cyclical and serves a purpose. Early humans, when they arrive, slot into that cycle like any other predator might. They influence the landscape in the way that beavers change the course of rivers. There were beaver teeth markings found in the wood beneath one of the manmade Mesolithic platforms at Star Carr. Before people arrived, the animals were using the site for themselves.

In this place even discarded timber has a strange and beautiful history. One piece of wood from the habitation site is like a baton being passed through time. In its first incarnation, before humans had arrived, it is a tree growing at the edge of the lake. The baton is then passed to the first inhabitants of the site, the Palaeolithic people, who split this piece of wood for their own purposes, and it was later embedded by the Star Carr people into one of the wooden platforms at the water's edge.

I am thinking of my dad who reused a curved stone moulding that he'd found in a skip, building it into his garden to create a pond feature. He did not know the people who had carved it, he did not know the house where it came from, or its purpose, but he was aware of them, and maybe this is the same, the same hunter-gatherer mentality, the same ingenuity with resources. First the forest, then the beavers, then the Early Stone Age, then the Middle Stone Age, all tracing their stories into the rings of the wood, all connected.

Here is the thin place where I can see the connection between myself and these far-away lake people; the place in which they become whole people, not simply points of history. It is not in the genetics, though of course we are all related to each other at some point in time, but in the thought processes around resources, the same way I have a cupboard full of plastic bags, a bag of rags, a box of handy used-and-cleaned ziplock bags, because I can imagine a way to repurpose them, because like many other people, I know the value of reusing objects for other purposes. The instinct to reuse and repurpose are the same, but for the people of Star Carr, the stakes were higher, the need to adapt quickly and find solutions to immediate problems might have meant the difference between life and death. I've always thought the thriftiness, the ability to see when something might have multiple functions, as being a kind of working-class legacy, bred from a time when any material object was precious and hard-won. Maybe it is simply a human thing.

Grahame Clark's explorations of the Star Carr site were short, three three-week summer digs between 1949 and

1951. Today the land is drying out to the extent that the ground has become buckled, twisting itself up like a badly sewn seam, but when Clark was digging it was still very much a waterlogged environment.

One of the earliest photographs from the site shows one of Clark's trenches with a huge birch trunk in the bottom, excavated precisely, but surrounded by sodden boards, the walls of the trench bowed and propped, and a cow peering over the edge, looking down at the work that is going on in its pasture. When Clark began digging at Star Carr, up to his knees in the oozing mud, bitten by horseflies, sticky in the heat and repeatedly having to drain the trenches, he discovered a site so rich with Mesolithic artefacts that for a while the Star Carr site held most of the Mesolithic artefacts ever found in Europe. Artefacts prone to decomposition – organic materials – are rarely found. But at Star Carr, the organic materials have resisted decay because they are beneath a layer of waterlogged peat that prevents oxygen from entering and therefore prevents the microorganisms that cause decay reaching these precious items. I think of the artefacts of my own life. If the landscape holds an archive of the lives lived on it, perhaps I am an archive for my own past lives. Perhaps the things that were elemental about me are not lost. Perhaps these parts of me that I have let sink and be covered and changed are anaerobically sealed, perfectly preserved under layers of the peat of my own life.

When Grahame Clark excavated Star Carr he found antler tools, bones, a wooden bow, a wooden paddle, a digging stick, and worked deer skull frontlets – strange skull masks or headdresses, the purpose of which remains enigmatic. The deer skull frontlets would become famous, emblematic of the site.

In photos from the time, the trenches look like opened arteries congealed with bones and wood, tree trunks and stone tools. It is like the ground itself is a body, and we keep opening its wounds to see how it works. I find the idea pleasing. I am trying to open my own self up to see how I work. I imagine peeling back a layer of myself to see what treasures are clogging my arteries.

At Star Carr there were thousands of pieces of bone. There were thousands of flints. There were hundreds of tools made from antler, along with some amber and shale beads, and perforated teeth which look like they might have been used as decorative items, perhaps jewellery. How human, to wear jewellery. Clark's trenches bled artefacts. An overwhelming amount of the Mesolithic came out of the ground at once, like a secret that had been kept for thousands of years, the keeper suddenly splurging. Later, archaeologists excavating with Dr Nicky Milner at the Star Carr site in 2015 found a beautiful shale pendant, decorated with mysterious lines. Tiny and fragile, probably unworn and yet deposited in the water, it has become as enigmatic as the deer skull 'masks'.

Perspective is key. Clark believed, because he had so little to compare it to, that the site must be entirely typical of the Mesolithic people, that this was probably a site where several small families passed through regularly, probably following migrating deer. It makes sense as a theory, until other sites of the same era are discovered. These northern European sites contained the same style of barbed hunting points, the same style of flints, but in nowhere near the same numbers as at Star Carr, and no deer skull headdresses either. Clark's archaeological work was well researched, carefully drawing together studies on seasonal animal behaviour and botanical life. There was keen observance and exploration of botanical residue in the examination of pollen found in trenches to add context to the excavation and the finds therein. It's rightly seen as excellent archaeology for its time. But it was still *of its time*. In the 1960s a bone was found on the shores of Lake Edward in Africa. There were twenty-eight notches in the bone. There have been many theories about what the notches might have meant, whether they were a form of agricultural measurement, a means of measuring food kills, hunting cycles, etc. In 1991 the ethnomathematician Claudia Zaslavsky suggested that a woman might keep track of her menstrual cycles by notching bone. Before this point, probably due to the male dominated nature of science, the idea that a woman might be one of the first mathematicians didn't register. Interpretation of archaeological evidence is constantly evolving, not just because of the evolution of technology used to assess artefacts, but because there is more diversity within the field, a greater range of perspectives and experiences. Similarly, what we would now consider to be an abuse of privilege, or at best poor practice, might have been the norm in a science still in its relative infancy. At the time of the first excavations at Star Carr, archaeology was still the bastion of the privileged white male, was still open to the abuses of collectors. Although the times were gone when 'gentlemen archaeologists' like Albert Denison could define which discoveries were and weren't important by imposing their own perceptions of the world, collectors were still finding ways to beg, borrow and steal, to buy, sell and benefit financially from antiquities and artefacts.

There are stories about this happening at Star Carr on at least one occasion, in 1950, when collector and colourful character Tot Lord, from the town of Settle, came to the site shortly before it was filled in. Tot Lord's grandson, Tom Lord, visited the site in 2016 and gave an interview for the Star Carr YouTube channel. In the interview he reveals how Tot Lord paid the workmen at Star Carr, who were tasked with filling the trenches, to go and have a 'good lunch' before helping himself to the artefacts left in the trench. He got on his knees in the mud while his friend waited to the side. Tot Lord dug his hand into the soft, waterlogged peat and began pulling out handfuls of antler and flint, throwing them up and out of the trench for his friend to gather. He worked his hand further into the black mud and felt a bear skull. Unable to pull the whole thing out, he did manage to work one canine tooth from the skull. It was only when his friend had an asthma attack, probably due to the fear of being caught committing such a heinous act, that he stopped. He took his finds home, dried them, slowly and carefully, and they ended up in Tot Lord's own museum – the Pig Yard Museum. Finds from the initial Star Carr site have ended up scattered around the world, making it very difficult to build a complete picture of the site.

Nothing was done at Star Carr for nearly forty years, when the Vale of Pickering Research Trust began their investigations. This project, which took place in the 1980s, involved a conglomeration of local businesses and archaeologists working together to fund digs at Star Carr and to explore the archaeology of the Vale of Pickering – the long, glacial valley area reaching to the town of Pickering, in which Star Carr sits at the eastern end – as a whole. They did a great deal of work around the lake site, which involved coring the earth to gauge where the lake edges had been. It is thanks to them that I, a complete amateur with nothing more than a special interest, can look up the shape of the lake on the internet and see where prehistoric habitation spots are around its edge. It is because of them that I can see myself in the story of the lake, and how I am connected to the lake people of the distant past.

In the 1980s the Research Trust undertook further excavations at Star Carr. The aim was to build on Clark's research and produce theories of their own about the use and purpose of the site. The findings were astonishing. They discovered that the site was much bigger than Clark had imagined. The Trust was able to divide the site into not just the muddy edges of the lake, but a substantial area of prepared dry land on which the Star Carr people had knapped flints and crafted the tools they needed to live and thrive in this environment. They found further worked wood platforms laid down along the edge of the lake. Like Clark's excavations, the work done on the site in the 1980s humanized the people living there. Like colourizing an old photo, these people and their lives became richer and more detailed.

This is where I enter the Star Carr story, not as an archaeologist, or even as a volunteer, but as a person living near the site whose childhood was affected by the information that filtered from the excavations, through to my primary school, and down through one or two special teachers to me.

I went to a primary school in Seamer village, near to the Star Carr site. We lived about a mile away down a long lane, called Long Lane. In the summer we would cycle to school, initially with me in a little red plastic seat on the back of my mum's bike, then with my own bike. The ride was one of fields and crab apple trees, ponies and stables and a terrifying, thickset bull who stood in a triangular field at the edge of the village like something from a Greek myth. As a teenager this was the road I walked home down, from the village where my friends lived, to the housing estate, through the blackest of nights. There are no street-lights on village lanes, no way of navigating other than straining your eyes to acclimatize to the dark, and using your knowledge of where you are in relation to certain trees, certain crops, the curve of the road. In those times, walking in the dark felt comforting, animalistic, senses heightened. I do this sometimes now, in my own village. I go out into the all-encompassing dark, the scent of mud and earth and grass in the air.

Very few people drove to school. There was no need, and the mindset was different then too: children were daily set sail into the world, to return after many hours playing in disused quarries, covered in skin scrapes and bruised from a day of climbing or attempting wheelies on their bikes. When I think back to the government warning films we trailed into the assembly hall to watch and be scarred for life by – the boy who lost his feet on the railway lines still haunts me now – I can see why these were necessary. For country kids our points of danger were drowning in lakes, crossing railway tracks, falling from trees and being chased by the bull.

I am trying not to romanticize country living as a kid, but there *is* something special about it, the total absorption of nature by a young mind, the way that you are still isolated, even if you can catch a bus to town. Not everyone who grew up in the countryside is attached to it, formed by it, but in my experience I don't know many people who aren't.

I have no idea what the school I attended is like now. The website is as slick and smart and compassionate as you would hope for, but without children of my own, the world of primary education is a foreign land to me.

When I attended the school in the 1980s, it was mainly made up of middle-class children, being taught by middle-class teachers. Perceptions of childhood experiences are difficult to unravel; what stings in childhood might still sting in adulthood, but only very briefly. But some experiences in childhood can leave a mark one carries into adulthood like a scar, and this was very much the case for me. Though I loved learning, loved reading, school was where I first felt like I didn't really fit in. I was a perfect package of oddness – a bit chubby, frizzy-haired, working class and, in hindsight, almost certainly autistic, though again, without the official diagnosis I hesitate to use the term. I don't know which of these were the most obvious. I felt like nothing about me was a good fit for any school situation, except that I was creative, I could draw, I wrote stories. That made me feel, if not part of things, certainly of value in some small way.

Autism can manifest differently in girls than in boys. For a long time, experts weren't aware that girls could present with different symptoms, and so many girls went undiagnosed or overlooked, likely feeling alienated but not knowing why. I didn't seek an autism diagnosis until I was forty-four, but since autism has been talked about more by people with direct experience, people like me – older women – I have realized that the signs were there all along. As I write this, I am still on the autism assessment waiting list. I am not sure why the diagnosis is so important to me, only that I feel it will be the final part of the puzzle.

The importance of a diagnosis is not so much about reaching support (there is very little official help, though I am aware there are charities offering advice) or changing how I live (it feels a bit late for that) but a diagnosis would, I think, help me to forgive and accept myself. If I know the landscape of myself, in the context of autism, it is like I am giving myself permission to be exactly as I am, and not blaming, controlling or trying to improve myself or instil value. My landscape, my oddness, is valuable as is.

When I first came to the idea that I might be autistic, I kept it in my periphery. I did not want the label. I did not want it because it would prove that there really was something 'wrong' with me. It would prove that I could not, however hard I tried, improve. I could not change. I would be fully on the outside, caged, unable to join in. I grieved for that.

Eventually, I realized that a diagnosis is not a cage. It is, in fact, the key to the cage. With a diagnosis, I could carry on my life simply being the way I am. It would give me permission to find ways to help myself, and to look back on my life and acknowledge that the sadness of my child self, and all her difficulties, were valid and acceptable.

A lot of my time spent in primary school was spent as a loner, singing to myself in the playground. I have a distinct memory of wearing a coat that I'd got from a jumble sale and marching round the perimeter of the playground singing in rhythm to my feet. The coat was a weird, 1960s (vintage!) leather trench-type coat with a fake fur collar. I loved the feel of the furriness against my face and even when my poor parents tried to get me not to wear it to school, because obviously it looked completely ridiculous, I refused to take it off. The coat disappeared from my wardrobe at some point in my childhood and never returned. At this time I had memorized every dog breed there was and could list them all. I told teachers that I was conducting research into the communication abilities of dogs. When I say I was odd, this is what I mean. You will know children like me, you will know adults like me: you will recognize them from old television shows from a time when 'autism' was not the term or diagnosis used to describe such behaviour. We are often the socially awkward professors, the library nerd girls, the scientists, sometimes we are the artists. As a child I was obsessed with nature. I would get books about nature from the library and copy the whole thing out by hand into a notebook. I struggled with socializing (I still do) and if I wanted to talk to anyone, I had to pretend to be someone else, I had to put on a metaphorical mask and hide my authentic self. I collected these masks from television and film characters, but my first mask was the companion I knew best, our family dog. Overwhelmed at school, I refused to talk, would only bark and sit under the teacher's desk. This went on for weeks until my parents were asked if I did this at home. But of course I didn't. At home I had my oddness vaguely mirrored back, was part of a tribe of eccentrics. I only recognized this behaviour for what it was in my forties.

In the early days of my research into autism, when I was writing about it in my diary because that was the only place I could admit to it, I saw a news segment on the telly: it was about the only British school for autistic girls. I can't remember anything about it, except that the children seemed so happy. It made me intensely sad for the little girl who grew into a woman who was sad for so much of her life.

Some of the teachers at that school provided a haven for me. One teacher, who I'll call Mrs M, was warm, funny, kind and a complete nerd for biology and history. I looked forward to reaching age seven and finally entering her hallowed classroom and a year of studying cow eyeballs, drawing Anglo-Saxon clothing, studying dinosaurs and writing stories. Some of the teachers were not as kind.

There were middle-class teachers who seemed to treat teaching working-class kids – especially the ones who quite obviously had less money – as something to be endured.

A few years ago there was uproar in the literary world over a writer who had described her life as a teacher in terms of what she could learn from her pupils. The book she wrote was celebrated initially, until several people pointed out that the stance of observing the pupils, even in the context of 'learning from them', might be problematic, and criticisms were raised asserting that the book contained racist and ableist descriptions of the children. To have a white, middle-class woman observing children who are working-class, ethnic minorities or neurodiverse as something to be observed and learned from smacks of privilege. From my own point of view, which is a working-class point of view, I recognize a familiar story. I sometimes think I walk into a room accent first. As soon as I speak, my northern-ness, my working-class heritage, is obvious.

There is often a well-meaning bias that is triggered when people hear a regional accent. There are stereotypes around accents. Some positive, some negative. For example, my North Yorkshire/East Yorkshire accent makes people automatically believe I am friendly and approachable, which is nice. But all through my school life and beyond, I have had my accent corrected. I've watched my friends have their accents corrected. This has rarely happened when I have had a teacher with a regional accent themselves. It seemed to happen when someone who spoke in a way associated with the middle and upper classes was teaching me. And while you can be middle class and have a regional accent, it's very unlikely that you would be working class and speak with received pronunciation. I know two people for whom this is the case, friends who have been given elocution lessons. It makes me sad that the expectations of society caused their parents to feel that one way to give their children a better chance in life was to change the way they spoke. The fact that this way of speaking has become the benchmark for the *correct* way to speak arises from a position of privilege. This is problematic. It assumes that the way you speak, the way your grandparents and parents speak, needs correcting. Your experiences, your accent and your world view are not *different*, they are *wrong*. And while this isn't the worst abuse of class, it is a little red flag, a tip of an iceberg that represents a bias that is threaded through higher education, through traditionally middle-class careers, through the arts and access to the arts and here, through access to landscape, to sites of scientific and cultural importance, to the places you want to walk, to your own story, your own existence.

The furore around the writer's book opened a wormhole of memories from this period of early childhood when the middle-class teachers joked about us, out loud, over our heads, and rolled their eyes when we didn't own the right kit or were unable to join in the conversations around pony clubs and ballet classes that they would have with middle-class students. When the rural kids talked about the young farmers' clubs, ploughing contests, their grand-parents' or parents' farms, they were mocked. Not in a blatantly cruel way, but in a way that cast them as some-thing different, interesting but funny, certainly not the norm, despite the school being in a village surrounded by farmland.

It was the teachers who made space for pupils to connect to their own landscape who had the greatest impact on me. It was in Mrs M's class that a boy – whose dad or grandad had an allotment relatively near the Star Carr site – brought flint arrow heads to the nature table. They had been dug up at the allotment, turned over in the dark, nutritious soil. He found so many that they seemed to me something almost ordinary. Like Grahame Clark and his perception of Star Carr as an ordinary Mesolithic site, my perception of the flints was skewed by how plentiful they were and how easy they were to find. I never imagined that, later, I would spend many years with my head down looking for flints in fields and never find one myself.

Mrs M took real interest in these items. She asked her expert friends and colleagues to identify them. She used the flints to teach us about the lives we were living. Anyone could find a flint in the soil if you were willing to dig – there was no step up that you were born with in order to claim that flint. That was important.

Years later, on a family holiday in my teenage years, I met a girl my own age and when I asked her what she wanted to do with her life, she said she wanted to be an archaeologist. I was amazed. I had never imagined that sort of career would be open to 'ordinary' people. I couldn't imagine anyone in my own family becoming an archaeologist. I certainly couldn't imagine myself doing that. Even though my dad was incredibly bright, an inventor slash builder, someone who was not afraid to go his own way to the point of being a bit eccentric, even though my parents had always told me I could do whatever I wanted if I worked hard, there was something missing which was knowing *how* to get to where I wanted to be. I didn't quite understand how to move from wanting to be something to finding the academic route to that point. I saw no one from my background doing the jobs I wanted to do. I went to schools where kids like me weren't really expected to do anything except be funnelled into local jobs – tourism, nursing, hairdressing, factory work – like pennies in an arcade machine. You have to see it to be it. And I did not see that. I didn't see working-class writers. I rarely saw working-class white-collar professionals. We didn't know people who were professionals. On the rare occasions when I speak about being from a working-class background and how that has impacted my career, it is difficult to explain this phenomenon, that often it is less about not having enough money and more about simply not seeing people with accents and backgrounds like your own working in the fields that interest you. I think this is changing. I hope this is changing. But it is a change that is created by working-class people building doorways where there were none.

Mrs M made my interests relevant rather than something else to be picked on for. She opened a door at a time when I had no escape from being me, and on the other side of that door were the Star Carr people, and the Anglo-Saxon folk from up the road at Heslerton, and the Romans from behind the quarry where I lived and the Palaeolithic people from the place we walked our dog. These were distant people, imaginary people, who I could connect with as if to ancestors. I am still doing this now. These were people I would never have to communicate with or make eye contact with or try to make excruciating small talk with. The Star Carr people knew nature and knew the land. They were like my people in that respect, like my grandad with his farm and my mum and her medicinal plants.

Very few people I knew were aware of the Star Carr site and their connection to it. According to a survey conducted by a team of archaeologists including Nicky Milner for a paper entitled 'The Meso-What? The public perception of the Mesolithic', only 8 per cent of respondents questioned in the nearby town of Scarborough knew the name of, or anything else about, the Star Carr site or the Mesolithic period. Only 3 per cent of people knew the name of the site, or what the term 'Mesolithic' meant. What is it that tunes the 3 per cent of people into this place? I feel it might be more than simply knowing of its existence. Perhaps people who are interested in and drawn to natural and social history of landscape are searching for a sense of belonging and connection.

In my family we talked often about our ancestry, about the people who had come before us. My dad's family in particular, and the thread of farmers before him, the ending of that long line in my dad, a bus driver. When I attempted to research my own family tree, years ago, I became frustrated by how many of the men were named after their fathers – John or Robert – and how many were listed simply as 'farm labourer'. They were the tools with which other people might make their mark in landownership, but not landowners themselves. I struggled to find their individuality and, of course, there was little else to research; they were working-class people leaving little mark on history. Their history, the stories of their lives, were passed down in the oral tradition. They are embedded in my accent. I carry them in my genes, I carry them in my very bones. I am perhaps still searching for my own ancestors, threading myself like a shale bead onto the string of my genes, further and further back down the line of our very existence. Like the archaeologists, I am also digging, but in a different way, like Seamus Heaney, with a pen instead of a trowel.

The most recent excavations at the Star Carr site began in 2004 and continued until 2015. It became apparent during research around the lake that the drying out of the land was impacting the artefacts. No longer were the antlers and bones coming up fresh and hard, they were now coming up spongy with a strange jelly coating. The peat was drying out and along with it the artefacts. Star Carr and any further knowledge of the people who lived there were at risk of being lost again. This time the archaeologists were from York University, with a team led by Professor Nicky Milner, who grew up in one of the local villages. They were on a mission to use every piece of modern archaeological technology to expand knowledge of the site.

When the digging was done, the conclusions were significant. This was not, like Clark had imagined, an example of a typical Mesolithic hunter-gatherer site, but rather a site of great importance, not just to us, looking down the long, inverted telescope of history, but to the Star Carr people themselves. One of their conclusions was that this was a key gathering place. It was a site that had been in use for at least eight hundred years, and generations of Mesolithic people had travelled there. They had continuously renewed and improved the area, maintaining the dwellings and expanding the wooden platforms, and they had been conscious of the previous generations and their impact on the site because they could *see* what they had left behind. They could see the work that their ancestors had done at the site, hundreds of years before, and they too left their mark on the landscape by continuing and adding to that work. They were aware of their ancestors, they were aware of their place at the edge of the lake, of their place in the connective tissue of the ecology around them, and it is most likely that this was a place of ritual behaviour.

The Mesolithic people of Star Carr, at the beginning of this era, may have just arrived in Britain, crossing

Doggerland, a now extinct land mass where the North Sea is, on foot. I can imagine them missing their home. I can imagine them searching for a way to belong. Perhaps this acknowledgement and awareness of previous generations by building on the platforms and dwelling places, the Star Carr site itself, were also acknowledgements of a story, of an ancestral route, something becoming more and more myth-like to them as the years passed.

Our modern perspective makes it difficult to understand the relationship between the Star Carr people and the land. They would no doubt know the landscape on a micro level – where every plant was, where every tree was, every danger, every resource. Nowadays we are a people encapsulated in vehicles; even when we walk and take pleasure in the environment it is as an act of observation. We would find the Star Carr people's closeness to the natural world a difficult relationship to understand because we have very few reference points. I can see it in some of my ancestors, especially the tenant farmers whose job it was to know the landscape intimately, but we cannot begin to imagine what it is to be a part of the environment in the way the Mesolithic people were. There are people out in the world who live this life, tribal people still connected to their own land ancestry, but most of us have lost that connection, and it cannot be reinstated. We can't re-wild ourselves. We cannot ever go back to a place in which we are fully integrated into nature. We can reconnect, we can find ways of being a part of nature, but it will always be like releasing cage-bred animals back into the wild. We have lost the ancestral chain that would tell us *how* to go back to that place.

With all the knowledge we have of the Star Carr site, experts are seemingly no further in understanding the purpose of one of the most incredible finds: the antler 'masks' or 'frontlets'. I can't remember the first time I saw one of the Star Carr masks. I expect my adult response would be much the same as my childhood response: the feeling of being watched by the masks is acute. I've been lucky enough to attend talks about the masks and to see one of them up close. The frontlets vary, some are more worked than others. Mostly they are deer skulls, with the 'face' removed to leave the top of the skull down to the nasal bone, with the antlers cut down to some extent. They are smoothed on the inside, and have holes bored into them which look like eye holes but are more likely to have been used to attach the frontlets to the head with twine. They are undeniably strange and eerie. Perhaps it is because I know that they have been removed from where they were specifically deposited, and that feels slightly sacrilegious. Or maybe it is the strangeness of the half-deer, half-human focus, that, if you take the bored holes in the skull as eye holes and get close enough, there is a thrilling fear that you may find someone looking back at you. These deer skull objects are the emblem of the site, featured on tea towels and keyrings in the British Museum. The frontlets are deer skulls, mostly red deer, but some are roe deer, and the earliest masks deposited at the site were elk. Even though the eye holes are not actually eye holes, and the masks are not facial masks, meant to sit above the face, they are still a kind of mask. Their purpose is still to change the appearance of a person, to make them seem unhuman.

The preparation of these frontlets is complicated. It's a process that archaeologists have been attempting to recreate for years, with a great deal of success. First the head is baked in a fire, the jaw of the skull is removed, the skin is removed, the bottom of the skull and the nasal bone are removed, the antlers are cut down, the inside of the skull is smoothed, and sometimes, but not always, two holes are drilled into the back of the skull. They are difficult to attach to the head. A face does not fit in the mask, a head does not fit in the mask, they cannot be worn like hats.

There are suggestions based on ethnographic descriptions of shamanic behaviour that these frontlets are attached to the head, with skins and twine, for animalistic ritual dances based around the hunting of deer. I can imagine that, in the light of a fire, a person might become the deer or become a half-human, half-animal form; they could exist between worlds and perhaps cross between worlds.

I have worn invisible masks all my life, mimicking those around me, characters in films and on TV, following the patter of language, the pauses, the way that people communicate with each other, to 'pass' as not odd. But my first mask, all those years ago in primary school, was the dog. I saw no reason why I could not simply become a dog. Of course, this is not a true comparison. But I feel like I know something about blurring the lines, about what it is to crave the very biology of another animal.

The careful depositing of the masks – as many as twenty-one in the original excavation, with that number rising in further excavations – in the shallow water around the platforms at the lake edge is believed to have been ritualistic. Water as a place of deposition is an important ritualistic element of the Stone Age onwards. Perhaps water, with its life-giving properties and its reflective surface, is the door to the underworld. When you throw a penny in a wishing well you are reaching back to this ritualistic practice. We can see it in the Roman gifts to spring water gods, we can see it in the Iron Age and Bronze Age bog bodies found all over Europe, the sacrificial act of relinquishing.

The careful work done by the archaeologists here, standing on the shoulders of archaeologists and amateurs before them, taught us so much about the site. The people fished, hunted, presumably used boats to get around. They brought flint down to the site from the Wolds to make their tools, but they also used the glacial till flint that was round and about. They made jewellery, like pierced beads and the shale pendant that was found with careful markings on it, one of the earliest examples of Mesolithic art. The people built tepees and cooked and ate and gathered. For eight hundred years. They kept dogs and hunted animals two or three times their own size, they felt the breeze that blew through the birch forest, and they touched the water with their feet. They lived here.

'It feels like a very familiar landscape,' says Professor Nicky Milner. 'I grew up near Hunmanby Gap, in the middle of nowhere really, but then when I did some research on my family tree, I found Milners in the graveyard at Folkton and could trace ancestors to Cayton.'

We are drinking tea in Nicky's King's Manor office in York. It is a small hive of activity, shared with Dr Jess Bates and Dr Charlie Rowley. There is no space left unfilled – the shelves are stacked with folders, files and replicas. There are three desks crammed in the space and, while we talk, Jess and Charlie are archiving. It is meticulous work. Each flint flake is being captured in a record, pinned down like a butterfly in a case with its identification and probable use. This is the sort of archaeology that would never make it into an Indiana Jones film.

Nicky has made the tea herself. It's decent – I can tell she comes from Yorkshire. Behind her chair hangs an artist's impression of how one of the Star Carr deer head-dresses may have been worn. I think it might be the drawing by Rebecca Strickson that appeared on a first-class stamp in 2017. It's beautiful: a line-drawn figure, who could be male or female, stands with their back to the viewer, their long hair spilling over the hint of a necklace, the hint of fur clothing. The headdress is worn on the back of the head, the twine threaded through the bored holes, tied round and under the chin. The artist has managed to capture a human being wearing the deer skull headdress, rather than the headdress wearing the human. Behind me is a whole case of 3D printed replica frontlets. I'm itching to handle them.

Nicky's area of research is the transition between Palaeolithic, Mesolithic and Neolithic. Her life's work has been Star Carr, a site that she has worked on for fifteen years. It's not a stretch to think of her as the leading expert on Star Carr. I have seen Nicky's name on articles and books, on archaeology-based TV shows and on course materials used by the University of York. I've been to talks where she has allowed the public to come up close to the artefacts. During one memorable behind-the-scenes museum talk we were able to handle one of the frontlets, smell the bark roll fire starters that had been excavated from the Star Carr site. It sticks in my head. I could smell the scent of the forestry around the lake and imagine it clearly just from that one small sensory experience.

The sensory experience of archaeology is important. We connect through the senses. As humans we navigate memory and imagination through the senses. As a poet, as a writer, I use sensory descriptions to convey images and feelings to the reader. It creates a deeper emotional connection. Think of how the smell of fresh cut grass takes you to childhood. The day I smelled the birch rolls and their piney, mossy, somehow fresh smell, I was able to imagine the lakeside, and a person attempting to start a fire, crouching on the flattened earth, behind the reeds, while geese flew overhead. One of the things I admire most about Nicky is her push to bring archaeology out of academia and to ordinary people.

'I remember visiting the Jorvik Viking Centre in York when I was a Brownie. Something I can really remember from the visit was being allowed to touch some pottery on a big wall display. You go to a museum, and everything's behind glass, but they were letting us touch the past. I think that was what got me into archaeology, really. That and I also remember a lesson we had at school, a kind of detective game with "Pete Moss, the Bog Man". You got a little card with all the archaeological clues on it, and you had to find the truth of who he was and how he died, how he had come to be in the bog. And I remember the feeling when the teacher said, at the end of the exercise, "But there's no answer. We don't know because it's archaeology." Because I felt like I was being a detective, and then it turned out that there wasn't actually a definitive answer. I can still remember that feeling. I wanted to know the answer.'

When I ask the three women what their impetus is, what it is they are looking for, what it is that keeps them digging, it's all about that strange place between the imaginary past and the actual past. The point at which you might bring from the earth an artefact last touched eleven thousand years ago. I imagine it like holding the hand of the person who left it there. 'It's like rebuilding that lost knowledge that you can't get from historical sources,' says Charlie. 'Like working-class communities, you'll find them in the archaeological record where they've been silenced in historical records, or completely lost, with prehistoric stuff.'

And what about the relationship between the archaeologist and the finds? This must be a special thing, to be the bridge between the past and the present, that must feel personal? 'I think people form attachments,' Jess says. 'You might only be digging for one season, but there's a real sense of attachment to the artefacts and to the place where you found them, so yes, it does feel personal.'

In the story line of Star Carr it's important, I feel, to recognize that the story isn't just about what is emerging from the ground. The mound of the rubbish tip in the background, for example, is the continuation of the story of the site, the drainage of the fields is part of the story of the site and the archaeologists themselves are a part of that story, not just as vehicles of interpretation for the previous inhabitants, but as human beings whose connection to the site and the Stone Age people is in turn influenced by what is happening historically in their own timeline. It's a wide, ethereal concept, that everything is connected and history cannot quite be pinned down in one place. Again, I get the feeling of time as being less linear than we accept. This is the story of the landscape and the archive that the landscape contains. How important is the imagination in reaching the people who might not even know they are part of the story?

Nicky is obviously passionate about the inclusive nature of archaeology, and how ordinary non-archaeologists who live on and by sites of special interest can be included. The two books she co-wrote, *Star Carr: A Persistent Place in a Changing Landscape*, volumes one and two, are accessible to people like me with no archaeological background. Nicky has also been involved in several free Star Carr online courses which again encourage discussion by people with no archaeological background, inviting them into this story. 'It depends on who you think your audience is,' she says. 'What we were trying to achieve with the Star Carr books and all the work that we did with that project was to make the archaeological research and interpretations more accessible, not just to academics. We wanted to make it more interesting than a lot of books that you sometimes get about these sites, because if you presented the information in a purely academic way, it would just be in a catalogue. But there *is* a stopping place, at the point where you're getting too far into speculation. I think we were quite careful in the way we used our language to say, *It could be this*, or *It could be that*, and to express our theories, why we are reaching the conclusions we are – we think these things because we're largely using ethnography to try and understand theories about the Mesolithic people in order to bring it a bit more alive.'

I return to Star Carr a few weeks after my visit with Mum. I am re-entering the story of this site. It is both my own childhood story and the story of people who lived here eleven thousand years ago.

I come first thing in the morning. It is now autumn proper. The weather is turning; it is wet, but it is mild. I have spent the intervening weeks between visits reading everything I can about the site, from the original dig reports to the latest studies, discussions, and conclusions. I have roamed the area in my mind's eye and on Google Earth, and I've looked up pictures. Something amazing has happened – I have become a time-traveller to the place. A lot of the data is beyond me – I am most definitely an amateur researcher – but occasional details open a world to me and bring me closer to the early lake people.

The people who came to the site likely arrived from the Wolds, or along the valley from the west. I have retraced their steps, walking down the slope from the Wolds, through a hollow way that is at least a thousand years old, into the valley below. This could be the route the Star Carr people took, or one similar, down the steep bank, zigzag-ging through the trees. I let my imagination run with the idea of them, imagine the story of these people, fictional-izing their arrival one day at the lake in autumn. I imagine them now, dressed in furs, sewn deer-hide trousers, a papoose for a baby, hide bags and baskets of flints and supplies carried on backs. It is a day like today: fresh, cool, the smell of the sea in the air. They come over the rim of the valley and the path opens through the woods. They look out and see, for the first time in months, the great rhythm of wind on the water of the lake. They drop down the path through the birch forest to watch and listen. In the distance an elk is calling, an unearthly sound. They feel the sound through them. They are entering a thin place of water, the underworld, themselves reflected in its surface. It is rutting season. The elk and the deer come down to the water's edge to drink. They will be as aware of the Star Carr people as the Star Carr people are aware of them. They are aware of the cracks of twigs and branches, the soft rush of wind in the treetops. They are aware of wolves here too.

One of the little ones is crying. It's his first time coming to the site. He has been excited about it for weeks, but now he is anxious. He's worried about the deer-man, he's scared of the water. His brother has told him that they throw annoying little brothers into the lake if they misbehave. This is the sort of language their mother chides. They'll have more reverence, she thinks as she watches her older son with his bow on his back and his broadening shoulders, once they see the platforms and can be near the water and their ancestors. At the lake site, the first party have arrived and set up camp. Already one of the men is seated on a log, knapping a good piece of flint he has found while walking. The sound of knapping flint is like the sound of glass falling on tiles, it chips sharp and cold in the air. A woman is watching her partner at the lakeside. He is crouching and stroking a hand over the crest of his best dog's head. Someone else is kneeling by a tepee, running a calloused thumb down the joints, looking around for a bit of wood or twine to tie the hide tighter to the base. The reeds are moving in the breeze. Even on a still day the reeds make a soft shushing. This is the sound they will hear while they sleep here. Within an hour or two the air chills, but the camp is prepared, the floors swept, the tepees patched up, cleaned out, fresh reeds have been laid, the furs unrolled and set down for sleeping on. The fire is lit. The dogs are excited by the prospect of bones and meat, their ears pricked to every sound. A skein of geese passes over, the party watch it come down near the island, the geese bobbing on the surface. They are home.

This time I know exactly where the site is. I walk along the edge of it. I stand and turn myself 360 degrees, imagining the platforms, the houses, a patch of flint debris left over from where someone has been knapping. The birchwood forest might be gone, but the slope up to the

Wolds is the same. There are still reeds and bullrushes growing along the drainage ditches. They whisper and shush in the slight breeze. There are still the occasional willows here, and birches growing where the water is highest. The Hertford River is a patchwork of green algae and swaying underwater reeds. Looking at the riverbank I can see, as John Moore must have seen, the different levels of striation, the black peat low down and beneath that the till of the glacier.

There is birdsong here, but also the constant noise of the A64, and over that, instead of the high, strange sound of the elk, the eerie sound of something industrial. The farm labourers are still gathering potatoes; the lorries are still reversing into loading warehouses. Every now and then I hear the siren of a door opening, the clang and clatter of metal on metal which echoes down the valley. Over towards Eastfield, the frozen chip factory belches steam into the air, creating its own clouds. A skein of geese passes overhead. Some things are different, but some things are not changed. I tell the people of this place that they are not forgotten.

# CHAPTER FIVE

# Flixton Island

It is months before I get out on a pilgrimage again. The first Christmas without Dad passes, and even with us rallying round to spend time with Mum she finds winter on the smallholding difficult. She struggles with the ice on the pond, with defrosting the car, with getting up and down the field to the chickens. All of it is done with the weight of grief on her, and my dad's absence hanging over the house.

Without Dad, the holiday period felt highly strung and overdone, as if we needed to prove that we could survive it. We went to Mum's with my sister and my niece. I made cocktails, and they were far too strong. It was nice to be with family, but it felt somehow lacking in substance. You have to grind through all those grief anniversaries at a time when existing without a loved one still feels abnormal. You can't do anything about it – you just have to live until their absence becomes normalized.

After the turmoil of a Christmas Day without Dad's festivity, and making sure that I didn't forget my daughter at the cemetery, when all the hum and fuss of the holiday period is over, I find myself craving the outside air and the open horizon, the feeling of the cold seeping into my lungs, boot soles on frozen ground.

I go seeking Flixton Island in early January, mid-winter, driving the winding road to Flixton village. I drive west, through sleet and icy rain, beneath the lip of the valley, the Wolds just out of reach. We've turned into the new year, and away from my dad and his life, and I feel it keenly; the grief is sitting with me as I drive. When I think about his death now, and in the future, it will be filed under 2022. He is shut into the year before. And we shall continue onwards.

Although it is mid-morning and the sun is up, it is a dim day, the light never quite illuminating the landscape. The bright yellow of farmhouse lights can be seen in the murk. As I turn into North Street, heading into the valley basin, I'm aware of a shift, a sloping down, as if I am sinking into the lake itself. Flixton is the middle village of a string of villages on the southern side of the lake site – Staxton, Flixton, Folkton – with Muston and Seamer bookending the east and west ends respectively.

Of the lakeside villages, I know Flixton the best, because of the Foxhounds pub, where my husband and I sometimes come for Sunday lunch. It is a great, sprawling old building, low-roofed and beamed, extended in every way imaginable, so that to enter it is almost to enter an underground cavern. It clings to the edge of the lake site and weighs history down like a paperweight. The interior is modern-meets-ancient, the old black beams juxtaposing the comfy velvet and leather booths and silvery wallpaper.

The names of the villages along this side of the lake site have always intrigued me. If landscape is the archive of place, then the names of places are the notes in the margins. Some people think the villages here are named after a family of Vikings, each son taking a village for themselves. Flix's town, Folk's town, Stax's town. It's a nice idea and I do like the image of these Vikings lining up along the side of the valley and naming their land, but it doesn't ring entirely true. In older maps, the village names are malleable, changing from map to map. This fooled me into thinking that Foulton was a place nearby, maybe a hidden village, an abandoned settlement. But it was actually the village of Folkton, reshaped by people whose spoken language I probably wouldn't be familiar with.

There is malleability to place names – they change with the language spoken, the language written, and they are sometimes only as substantial as the person saying them. A place can be multi-named, but very rarely nameless. Even the fields have names. Sometimes our familiarity with a place can manifest in a casual renaming of it. When I talk about living in Bridlington, I say Brid. 'Brid' is the familiar, slightly scruffy unapologetic town of my early adulthood. 'Bridlington' is the place that tourists visit. For me, the word 'Brid' sits like a loom weight, holding down a tapestry of good and bad memories. I don't know Flixton well enough to know if it has a colloquial name.

It's true that there are a lot of Viking place names around this area, but even those names tend to refer to what the land is known for, what commodities the local folk found useful, what they might have traded in. I'm no expert on Viking terminology or history. I know only what I've seen and what I've read. Maybe the villages here are named after the crops that grew in the area, maybe they are named after the flax that was grown in the fields, or fleece shorn from local sheep, or maybe the names are rooted in even older lore. In Old English, to be 'Flax Fóte' is to be web-footed. Perhaps the people here were known for their watery lives.

I am thinking about the familiarity of a place, this place, and how often I have driven past the village, visited the pub here, but how I have never really walked around the village itself. The feeling of familiarity is at odds with my anxiety over doing just that – having a walk through the village. I am trying to be bold. But right now I can feel my confidence is bruised. My sense of belonging is unsettled again, perhaps due to my dad's death. I feel out of place. But still, I have promised myself a pilgrimage, a journey, and I have made a commitment to understanding the place where I live and actively belonging to it. Right now I do not feel like I should be here. I feel like a freak. I am not a natural explorer. I find it difficult to exist outside of what one might perceive as the safety of familiar surroundings. It is when I go to places where I feel I might not 'fit in' that I struggle. When I see photographs on social media of fellow writers climbing mountains and disappearing over the gravelled lips of caves and caverns, I can't help but compare myself and my steady, plodding manner. I have never been a conqueror of anything. But I do push through and survive, and perhaps that's enough. If you want to be a true explorer, you have to be able to own your place in the world, to know you are meant to be wherever you are meant to be, even if that is on a path that isn't marked on a map, or one that you are not sure is private property, a right of way, a bridlepath, a fine, chalk track you think you can see but then aren't sure when you get onto it. That has never been me.

I am the sort of walker who looks at the map a hundred

times, who checks the area on Google Earth, who drives past the start of a walk so that I know where I am going. But since the death of my daughter, since everything became different, since I decided *not to sweat the small stuff,* or rather the small stuff became so completely insignificant next to her death, I have tried to push through my hesitance, to tell myself I have a place here, that I too am worthy of being in the landscape I grew up in, that I belong, even if I feel that I don't.

The idea that we must conquer nature, that we must climb the mountain, we must swim the channel, we must force ourselves into the world and own it, is a kind of brutalization, born of fear perhaps, in the way that westerners once felt we needed to colonize the world, rather than exploring on equal terms. I am aware that I am simplifying something enormously complex.

This morning, on the news, there were reports of more deaths from extreme weather, more backtracking on environmental legislation. I feel anxious and hopeless, and I keep having to remind myself that I cannot change how others react around nature, but I can change how *I* react to nature and the landscape. Simply to engage with nature and to tell others what that feels like, perhaps that might be enough. I don't want to conquer. I want to explore. But I want to explore with a small e.

When I get out of the car on North Street, my self-consciousness manifests as a concern that someone might see me and think me a criminal. I need to keep reminding myself that I am allowed to walk here, that I am not the grinch come to steal the gifts from these beautiful, expensive houses still brightly lit with Christmas lights. I am aware that this neighbourhood is the community of a different type of person, a different tax bracket, and that

I am not a part of that level of society. Perhaps this also has a part in making me feel out of place.

The thing about being from a working-class background is that even if you are socially mobile, you never quite leave it behind. I suspect that even if I won the lottery and could afford one of these houses, the feeling of otherness would never go away. So far, working in the arts, my experience is that it doesn't matter how well my work is reviewed, how highly I scored in my MA in Creative Writing (distinction), how many people enjoy my courses and workshops or how many competitions I win, I will still have my accent commented on, still be talked to as if I am an anomaly, a source of interest because of where I come from and the direction I have taken to get to where I am. And although these experiences are in the minority, just a tiny percentage of my experiences in the generally welcoming and vibrant creative community, they stick, they sting, they have affected my confidence.

Maybe I need a thicker skin. Maybe I am oversensitive. I suspect the coat of working classness that I carry over my arm at all times would still be in the boot of my lottery winner Jaguar. *Different is not the same as less than*, I tell myself. I want to take control and internalize that message, not the one that I heard in my teenage years when I wanted to escape the boundaries and confines of my small world and be *someone*. The impression I got was to think like this was to be snobbish, and up myself. I internalized that guilt. And I didn't reach for those things.

I am fiercely loyal to my working-class background, proud of it, and not just because I've had to work hard to be accepted into an industry in which my accent is still a novelty, but also because that community gave me my moral compass. It's my family, my ancestry, and it forms part of my identity. This pride sits alongside the guilt in attempting to better myself. It feels embarrassing to want more. The perception, my internalized perception, of bettering myself is to move into middle-class-dominated arenas feels problematic. *Different is not the same as less than.* I have this mantra in my head alongside a voice that says, *Who do you think you are?* The whiplash I get from listening to them both is exhausting.

I was always creative, but a career as a creative was almost unheard of in my community. Creative activities were seen as hobbies. It's too hard to make a living from them, and perhaps the community I came from knew in very real terms what happened when you couldn't make a living from your line of work. I can hear my mother gossiping with her sisters about the folk in the town she came from – people she knew from school falling away because of a mistake, an investment gone wrong or an unexpected bairn on the way, or someone daring to try their hand at something insecure. *'They're in Queer Street now.'*

When I realized that creativity was an essential part of my identity, and I made a commitment to abandon the nay-saying voice in my head and went seeking the work that fulfilled me, I landed in a foreign country. I found a place with a different landscape, a different language and I struggled to find my way. The industry seemed metropolitan – it was slick and careful and well designed. It was London-centric. I had never imagined I could enter this place, *the arts*, because the doorways had been somewhere else, more readily opened to people from other backgrounds. I don't want to portray myself as some sort of stereotyped northern working-class hero, accomplishing my dream *despite* my background. Because I aren't, and I didn't. My point is that there should be no 'despite' about an ordinary working-class person working in the arts, whether that's as a writer, a facilitator, a professional, a publisher. But I'm also aware that I claimed my small stake in that world because I made my own doorways. It turned out that although there were lots of gatekeepers and locked doors, the walls were actually not very substantial. They could be kicked through if you were gauche enough to do that. However, by doing that, I made it even harder to be accepted. Instead of, for example, waiting to be invited to run courses and workshops based on my career as a writer, I decided to play to my strengths and set up my own workshops and courses, aimed at helping people from 'non-traditional backgrounds' into the arts.

My workshop attendees, the people I mentored, were mostly older, mostly women who had spent their lives attending to the needs of others, coming to the joy of writing and shyly offering me their poems. It was good work, it was nourishing work, and it was hard work. I had to keep my prices low to be able to facilitate working with people on low incomes, and by doing that I remained on a low income myself. But I wanted to *work* in the arts, not just experience snippets of that life while I worked on a production line or at a laboratory bench labelling pots of piss. Even with three degrees and a reputation for high-quality facilitation, even with competition wins to my name and celebrated poetry collections, the work opportunities available to me in the arts were often pitifully paid and aimed at people who already came from money. Who can afford to work for free as an intern? Who can afford to work for less than minimum wage (once preparation time, travel expenses, time spent answering student emails and marking, etc., is taken into consideration) facilitating workshops, working with people who might need more help to achieve their goals? People who are doing funded PhDs and need to top up their income while gaining experience. People who already have an income and for whom this sort of work is almost a hobby. These people were rarely people from working-class backgrounds.

The houses in this part of Flixton are very old, some of them at least as old as the seventeenth century. There are newbuilds too, built in keeping with the style of the area. The houses here are made of chalk, a hard Wolds chalk, framed by red bricks. In every village on the south side of the lake, the houses are built this way, and out towards the coast, and up on the Wolds too. Anywhere where people can pull building material out of the earth, they have. Just up the road between Muston and Folkton, like an eye socket carved into the valley wall, is an ancient chalk quarry, perhaps from an era as distant as the Neolithic. The long barrows in the area, especially those that stood proud on the valley top, were chalk coated and must have shone like celestial bodies under a bright moon. I have seen the way that chalk seems to glow in the dark. Perhaps their purpose was a dual one – helping the local folk find their way home in a place of absolute darkness and remembering the dead in their own darkness. The barrows here are all ploughed out to nubs and stubs now, and, like the lake, only visible to those who know what they are looking for and have a good imagination.

In my fleece-lined, waterproof trousers, heavy winter coat, bobble hat and scarf, I feel like a deep-sea diver submerging through striations of light, searching for the absolute bottom of the lake. As I walk, the houses begin to peter out behind me, the constant sound of the A1039 begins to fade at my back as the road changes from North

Street to Flixton Carr Lane. I am sinking into a landscape of farming. The road becomes edged by two ditches, probably drainage ditches, but also likely boundary ditches – the separators of parishes. The ditches are lined with trees – hawthorn, willow and a line of impressive old alders, their roots exposed and clawing into the bank, their twisted branches grasping the last of last year's catkins which hang red and straggly on the ends of their limbs. Alders are a sure sign that water is nearby. The village has opened out to fields, some neatly enclosed in modern electric fences, some with the vestiges of old hawthorn hedges streaking across them. Initially there are allotments and a horse stable in which I can hear someone mucking out, the steady rasp of shovel under shit, the background noises in rural places.

I have a sudden memory of a day like this one, maybe seven, eight or even nine years ago, sitting in my car at the top of this lane, waiting for a horse owner to come out from one of the stables and bring me a fresh bag of horse poo to examine under my microscope. I did this as a job for a while, alongside dog walking. On that day I was sitting and listening to the rain running down the windscreen, seeing the fields and the lake site emerging and disappearing, distorted by the water. I was working for myself, my own boss. But I was still a bit lost, still a bit bruised from the loss of my daughter, the continuing IVF treatments, the miscarriages. It's such a strong memory that I stop and close my eyes for it, letting it play out in my mind. I can feel it – the damp cold of the car, the heaters panting to warm the space, the bone tiredness of that time.

Back in the early years after my daughter died – after more IVF, more losses, a long-drawn-out investigation into her death which resulted in the devastating news that she might have been saved, that we were let down, that *she* was let down – I found myself no longer able to work in the hospital in which we had received substandard care, and where that substandard care, that clinical negligence, had been proven to be a factor in me no longer being a parent, in me never being a parent. I had worked there in the pathology laboratory first as a technician, then through the completion of a part-time biomedical science degree, generously funded by the NHS trust. I had worked my way up to the role of microbiologist.

My parents had a strong work ethic and taught me never to turn down an opportunity to better myself profession-ally. Even though I think I knew at that point that microbiology might not be for me, I was drawn to the idea of pulling myself up, doing better, being better, being one of those women that beauty magazines were always angled to, *professional* women with make-up and haircuts and smart trouser suits. You never see factory worker chic in *Vogue*. I worked in the lab for thirteen years. I never once wore a smart trouser suit while I was there. And if I had, it would have been under a Howie coat – a lab coat that fastened right up to the neck and right down to the wrists. Did I enjoy the work? Yes. I liked helping people, I liked being a part of a machine in which the patient was at the centre. I liked being a part of the NHS. But there was a lot that I didn't like too.

There were a lot of things that came together and caused me to leave the lab and my family of lab workers. Grief had destroyed everything that had been normal about my life. There was no returning to it. It affected how well I could work. I found that when it was time to return to work after my daughter's death, and do a job that paid well and had a good pension scheme, I couldn't. Added to this, each miscarriage floored me, each IVF cycle destroyed me, each stage of the investigation into my daughter's death eviscerated me. I was wrung out from grieving. Every day became an obstacle course. I was living a life so far away from normality, so far away from the life I'd had before, that I felt like I wasn't a real person. I longed to be set free, and freedom was this – animals, outside, weather.

The last couple of months of maternity leave, when I was preparing to return to work, were spent in an agony of anxiety. After my maternity leave ended, I struggled to go back into the laboratory building itself. I struggled to stay in one physical place. Time had become unstructured. I time-travelled between the ward where things had gone wrong with my pregnancy, and the place in which I was a working member of the team, needing to be switched-on, competent. I would find myself staring at the wall, spaced out, reliving my emergency c-section. I wouldn't be able to tell you how long I had been away from myself. Small things took me back to that time immediately after the loss – the sound of a fan turning, the smell of disinfectant, the soft hum of voices. At lunchtime I would sit crying in the car rather than go into the building and sit with people whose lives had just carried on, the inevitable pregnancies and births, the inane chatter in the break room. It wasn't like that constantly, and I did make progress in getting back to 'normality', but the problem was that the impact of this traumatic loss had destroyed what was normal. There was no normal to return to, just a jigsaw of shrapnel and the impression of the life I used to lead.

Every loss I experienced after that point threaded back to that initial atomic bomb of losing my daughter. I didn't have time to heal because we were straight back to IVF treatments. I dragged a heavy clock around with me that counted up the days since losing my daughter and counted down the days to menopause.

When the investigation revealed just how many things had gone wrong with our care, I became completely paranoid about making any sort of mistake at work and causing the same pain to someone else. I became convinced I was somehow a talisman of baby-death and couldn't bear to be around pregnant women in case I somehow infected them. Sometimes my body took over, like a guardian angel, and I would find myself driving straight past the hospital and, instead of heading into work, instead of driving into the car park and getting out of my car and walking into the laboratory, I would simply keep going. I would simply *not* turn down the road, *not* park in the car park. I just wanted to feel a little bit of the experience of *not* putting myself through that every day, not having to build armour and wear it for eight hours. I'd end up on the moors, driving towards Whitby, feeling a thrill of freedom in my chest. No, not a thrill, a *relief.* But then that little tickle of responsibility would kick in, that feeling of guilt, that feeling of letting people down, of knowing I needed to pull myself together and get on with it, that everyone goes through tough times, I wasn't special, I was weak for not being able to handle it. I'd pull into a passing place, turn the car around and head back, the weight of the day ahead settling like a cannon ball in my stomach.

There is only so much pulling yourself together you can do before you start to turn yourself inside out, split your stitches, break. In short, I was broken, suffering from PTSD and repeated bouts of severe depression and anxiety, and eventually, one day, I couldn't do it anymore. One day I left for real. I walked away. Literally, I got up from the bench, got up from my microscope and walked out of the lab, the hospital and just continued walking. I rang my husband as I was striding away from the town, walking over the rise, looking out over the cemetery and the hospital, and I told him I was done. I am aware of how utterly inconvenient it was for my teammates, and I carry that guilt with me, but I had exhausted everything and I couldn't do it anymore. When I look back now, I don't know how I did it at all. I wish I could go back, as the person I am now, and protect myself. I wish I could go back and advocate for myself in front of the panels of NHS HR representatives and laboratory bosses who had standards to meet.

Once I had experienced that animal grief, abandoned the rules of society and allowed myself to be consumed by it, how could I then zip back into my human skin and belong in a world of microbes and antibiotics and work schedules and staff nights out, all the things that had meaning and value to me in the before time? Even writing this, in my office at the break of dawn, where the jackdaws have just flown past the window to their daytime roosts, where all is peaceful, thirteen years after my daughter's death, nine years since I stopped working at the hospital, six years since the last IVF treatment, I can feel the terror, anxiety and grief building, I can hear the fan turning in the hospital ward where we sat with my daughter's body.

When I ground myself – by watching the trees outside my office move in the breeze, by watching the magpie on the fence, its head tilted as it examines the last shrivelled berries on the bush, by looking out to the ridge of the valley wall and seeing the sun returning, as it has done for millennia, as people have watched for thousands of years – I remember I am not there. I no longer need to be that square peg in that particular round hole. I am making my own place to be. Sometimes it is enough simply to exist in time. And here we are, here I am, a writer, telling my story to you, in a published book. My dream has come true. My pain, my experience, is a part of me, it is embedded in me like a piece of broken glass. I run my finger along the scar and feel for it like an old friend. I do not need to conquer anything; I just need to exist and experience it. I think about this as I pass the stables and smell horses and dung and sweat and leather and say a silent prayer of thanks to the universe that I am no longer forcing myself to work through PTSD, and no longer hunched over the microscope in my kitchen, surrounded by horse poo, bleaching my worksurfaces until they began to disintegrate.

After I had left the hospital and was no longer a microbiologist, I set up my own animal care business including horse faecal parasitology. From this point I gradually took on more and more writing and workshop facilitating work until the day I decided to close down my animal care business and settle to the thing I'd wanted to be so long ago, a writer. I regret nothing of the path that I chose to get here, each situation, each experience, had a set of lessons to teach me. Some of them were life-affirming, some of them were warnings. It took a long time for me to value my own skills.

There are more people about than I expect. North Street and Flixton Carr Lane must be popular dog walking routes. I am greeted repeatedly by small dogs and big dogs. As I pass a farm that breeds Hereford cows, a small family appears – two toddling children and, presumably, their dad, all in wellies and overalls, with a dog that looks like Tintin's Snowy. The little dog is immediately on me, licking my hand and running between me and this little family as they laugh and attempt to call him back. They're going the opposite way, heading up to the village. The landscape is one of wet and cold, but still there is a flock of starlings and fieldfares making their way industrially across the grass in one field, and high above a buzzard is being harried by crows. I watch them with my binoculars, then turn to look for the elusive roll of land that is Flixton Island. Flixton Island is one of several raised areas in the Paleolake Flixton site that would have been islands at the time when the lake was a true lake – a body of water. It's thought that the Mesolithic people of Star Carr might have hunted on these islands, using small boats to row across the water. During excavations of Flixton Island, evidence of Palaeolithic people and their lives has been discovered.

This is not the first time I have driven down this lane to seek Flixton Island. Years ago, while I was still working at the hospital, I spent a day as a volunteer on an archaeological dig of this place. I was late on my first day, my anxiety had got the better of me, and I'd spent too long paralysed by it, frozen in the doorway, my desire to be at this dig, to do something I'd always dreamed of, fighting against my social anxiety and my desire to crawl back into bed where it was safe. My desire to be at the dig won and I followed the directions down the lane, horrified that I would have to drive over the narrowest of bridges to get into the field.

The day was hot, and I was unfit. My knees creaked and ached from bending, and I had to keep turning my ankles to bring life back to them. My back felt hunched and crumbling from kneeling in the mud. I was surrounded by, mostly, nineteen-year-old students who leaped in and out of the trench we were working in, lithe as gazelles, while I maggotted my way along the ground, a big old lump. I worried that I might accidentally throw something away that was incredibly important. As far as I know, I didn't discard anything that should have been in a museum. After a while of this steady work, moving in a line up the trench like grazing cattle, my mind settled into the rhythm, and it felt good to feel the light and shade of clouds passing over the trench. It felt good to hear the skylarks and to be embedded in the landscape, quite literally. I became a kind of conduit, the place where the ancient past was meeting the present, and I felt emotional, deep inside, and also somehow away from myself. I felt like a bird looking down on myself. It was a completely unique experience for me. I felt I might do something mad like start talking to the earth or try to communicate with long-lost people. I wanted to be gentle with the earth, here, as we were unpicking it.

We peeled the black peaty earth away, thin layer by thin layer, so gently, so delicately, as if we were surgeons operating on the ground. And as we worked our way down, the earth began to tell us its story. We could see the recent plough lines just under the turf, their wave formation across the field. Further down were the medieval plough lines, and further still were the sedge, the reeds, the ghost lake, and then out of another gravelly white layer, a sudden scatter of half-moons; horse hoofprints emerging from the ground. These were late Palaeolithic or early Mesolithic hoofprints from horses long extinct. Short, stocky little horses, truly wild horses that had come to drink at the edge of the long-gone lake. I felt the physicality of their presence, imagined I could smell the dungy, sweaty scent of them. Time had become thin enough to reach through and touch the stiff bristled mane, smell the grass on their breath.

As the dig ended for that day, a discovery was made in another trench. Horse bones. Butchered horse bones. This, then, was a hunting site where late Palaeolithic or early Mesolithic people had come to kill the horses where they drank. The bones were a rusty red colour. To my untrained eye, they looked like red sticks or tree roots. But these bones, with their butchery marks, were stacked neatly together, and deposited in the ground, or the lake, by the people who had hunted here. There was such gentle reverence in the act. The *reverence* of the act moved me. It spoke to me about the relationship between food and man, animal and man.

The land around Flixton has a long history of farming development. It has been conquered in the name of farming. This place was once fenland. Fenland is lowland, marshy land, prone to flooding. The process of transforming from a lake to fenland was gradual: over thousands of years the lake slowly began to fill with reeds and the reeds became peat and the ground became liquid in places, boggy in places, solid in places. It existed in this watery state for hundreds of years.

When you say the word 'fen' or think of 'The Fens', you might automatically think of the east of England, Lincolnshire, Cambridgeshire, Norfolk. But Yorkshire was fenland once too. The Yorkshire fens stretched north of Lincolnshire for 3000 square miles. This fenland was still part of the landscape four hundred years ago, in the sixteenth century, and in some areas well into the eighteenth century. In some places the fenland was so watery that villages were like islands within it. The people living in this complex environment were tuned to it, skilled in the ways of gathering, surviving. You can't see this fenland environment anymore – it's lost to drainage now – but it is there in the named places. Every place marked with 'carr' – from the old Norse *kjarr*, meaning wooded marsh – is an indicator of the landscape, its history and its people.

The people of Paleolake Flixton would have been tuned to their watery environment. The uncontained River Hertford, running in its natural state through the middle of the lake site, fed the wetland, flooding regularly and spilling silt into the spongy earth, the meadowlands, providing a nutritious base for hay growing. At this time, anywhere that couldn't be used for arable farming was classed as 'waste' or common land. Common land was open to the common people, the cottagers and villagers. The people used the fenland – they fished it, they hunted waterfowl, they gathered the plants that were useful, like willow and thatch.

It is difficult to imagine exactly how people lived, how different life was in this period, right up to the eighteenth century. Again, I think of the hunter-gatherers of Star Carr, the horse hunters of Flixton Island, and I can see a bridge between them, stretching also to the eighteenth-century villagers who lived on the fenland.

The fenland in this area would have been utilized alongside farming systems that had been in place for hundreds, maybe even thousands of years. This started to change gradually as land began to be enclosed by those with the money and power to do so. A typical village, like Flixton, in the medieval period onwards, would have had a manor with enclosed, private grounds, but also land owned by the manor that was common ground. Some version of an open field system would have been in use for the villagers. These systems were varied and based around landownership but were communal places. Within the open field system, strips of land were divvied out. The strips were

111

spread between different areas so that everyone had a chance to use good quality land, as well as the less productive land. No one was lumbered with only unproductive soil. There would have been a hierarchy running through this system. The lord of the manor was always the biggest landowner. Below him would be any non-gentry, wealthy landowners, then those who paid their tithe to use the land strips, and below those the people who, by disability or circumstance, were not able to work the land. These people were reliant on charity and the church. The farming of land was a community affair. To plant new crops or bring new farming practices into use, all the community had to agree to them.

People with no land, the poorest of the poor, still had a legal right to access common land. It was open to all, and there was more to it than simply being a place for cattle to graze. Medicinal plants were gathered from meadows. Berries and fruit could be foraged. Hedgerows, many of which contained fruit-bearing trees or bushes, played a hugely important role in supplementing the diets of the people living around the fenland, and they also provided fuel for fires and stoves. Run well, the system provided autonomy and a sense of purpose – the people worked for themselves and gave a portion of their profit in exchange for more land to work and houses to live in. They used the common land as a means of enriching their diets and their income.

This changed gradually. Any expert on the history of land enclosure will tell you that it is complicated and to polarize it with a simple right or wrong argument would be oversimplifying an extended period in which communities felt differently about land enclosure depending on whether they benefited from it or not. But it is impossible not to have some sort of opinion on it as you dig deeper and realize just how much impact the gradual removal of common and communal ground had on poorer, working-class people.

I am not an expert, and I find the timeline of enclosure challenging; the laws and motives of those bringing in regulations and rules are difficult to comprehend from a distance. What I understand of it is that between the thirteenth and twentieth century, enclosure of lands began to occur. It happened by choice, and it happened by force, but put simply, the people with power – the monarchy, the landlords and the lords – systematically reduced the land that working-class rural people could exist on and had access to. The common land was gradually privatized. The first moves towards this privatization of land perhaps began with the Statute of Merton in 1235, a law that allowed large landowners and lords to enclose land that was directly around their manor houses for private use. Previously, although they were the beneficiaries of the land, it was still open to use by the community. At this time, a person tended to own the rights to the land, or to certain aspects of the land, and movable property on it (e.g. animals) but the land itself could still be accessed by the public. Factors that led to this gradual privatization of common land included the price of British wool increasing, and therefore the value of good grazing land increasing. Why grow barley or wheat when you could farm sheep? It was more profitable to graze sheep and sell the fleece than it was to take a percentage of what the villagers could grow on that land.

As the land available to the working classes shrank, so too did their incomes and livelihoods. Evictions occurred where lands were to be enclosed. In small towns and villages across Yorkshire, people were left homeless. Records show that Wharram Percy, the abandoned medieval village on the Wolds, suffered a series of evictions due to land enclosure. Records also show that during the Tudor land enclosures, common folk on the Wolds rioted, attacked the enforcers, broke down fences, forcibly continued to graze cattle on the common land. But here in the valley, on the edges of the ghost lake, the transition, at least towards eighteenth-century enclosures and drainage, appears to have been carried out with little resistance.

It is, of course, difficult to tell how local, working-class people felt during the periods of land enclosure. Their voices come through in lawsuits, in court records, in newspaper articles about the riots. But otherwise, they are silent in history, unrecorded and marginalized.

The biggest wave of land enclosures occurred between 1750 and 1850 through Acts of Parliament. Remaining land and strips of common land were enclosed, and while working-class people were given other strips as compensation, these were generally of poorer quality. The 'waste lands', i.e. the common lands, were also enclosed. By the end of the nineteenth century, the common land, so essential in supplementing the lives of the rural working classes, was now enclosed. By 1940, according to the UK Parliament, 5200 enclosure bills had been enacted. Around 6.8 million acres had been enclosed, a fifth of the total area of Britain.*

Pheasants, introduced to Britain in the eleventh century, became popular as a bird to hunt in country sporting pursuits in the sixteenth century. Pheasants used the hedgerows for shelter, and because of this, use of hedgerows by

---

* Enclosing the Land – UK Parliament, www.parliament.uk/about/ living-heritage/transformingsociety/towncountry/landscape/over view/enclosingland/

common folk was restricted. With the hedgerows protected for game, people were no longer allowed to collect firewood from them, or gather the fruits, berries and nuts that grew in them lest they disturb the birds. People were driven away from a life of autonomy and into a life of servitude: the working-class rural folk began to work for the land-owners, taking a wage and cultivating the land for others to profit from, with no way of subsidizing their income from the lands that they lived on.

In the nineteenth century, in Flixton and the lake area, the landscape of the lake was changed further. A deliberate and complex process of drainage began that saw the river rerouted into straight canals. The land was drained, to be used instead for agriculture. The fenland disappeared, and the wildlife – the bitterns and eels and wild fowl – were gone. The common land, and a way of life entwined with the fenland, was gone forever, along with a connection to the landscape that couldn't be replaced.

The people born and living in Flixton, as well as their parents and their parents' parents, would have known this landscape intimately. They would have known what to gather, what to hunt, the life cycles and behaviours of the animals that came here and were hunted. Sometimes this repurposing of the landscape was done with a drive for production – with more arable land, more crops could be grown and more people could be fed – but in reality the process was slow going. Rent went up as the land became more 'valuable'. People left the villages.

Back at Flixton, at the end of Carr Lane, a bridge takes me over the diverted River Hertford, a slick glassy slab between bare banks. Mid-winter, nothing growing, nothing swimming. The wind whips over the surface, rippling the water. I stand on the bridge and turn myself like the point of a compass, listening for the sounds of the carr which are, today, distant industrial sounds of metal on metal, lorries reversing, but mainly the wind, mainly the sound of air passing over the landscape, mainly the sound of reeds moving, bare hedges and trees whining in the cold.

Past the bridge another island, this one more prominent – No Name Hill. No Name Hill was excavated recently. They found similarities to Flixton Island, but no horse bones. I walk on, past fields and looking over to the other side of the lake site and the industrial landscape of factories and the secondary school I attended in Eastfield. The valley on the north side of the lake site is less defined, it begins to spread and splay and break away, the tabular hills rising from smaller culverts and smaller valleys that wind away to Scarborough and east to Filey.

When I turn back and look where I have come, I suddenly get a clear perspective – I can see Star Carr quite clearly, the tree line along the edge of the field beneath which the site sleeps. Flixton Island is in the foreground, barely visible, but definitely there, a sort of wave or ripple of land rising from the Hertford. The Star Carr people would have seen the islands from their camp. But the Star Carr people never knew the horses that were killed here.

These horses disappeared from the area a few hundred years before the Star Carr people arrived. This is probably due to the landscape altering. The wide savannah of the post-glacial valley began to change to woodland, the horses moved away, and deer filled the space. It gives me shivers to think that the people who came here were around even earlier than the Star Carr people, and I can't help but wonder whether they were related. I think of the oldest photo I have of my farming ancestors, a picture of my great, great, great grandad from 1911. A hundred and twelve years ago. My grandad could remember the Victorians of his family, a link of genes that becomes more and more delicate through generations. The people themselves are remembered through their actions and interactions. Did the Star Carr people talk about a time when their ancestors hunted horses in the way I talk about a time when my grandad drove shire horses over the fields?

There is a bench at the end of the road before the tarmac peters out into a footpath. It looks like it might have been placed there fairly recently, and it looks functional rather than comfortable. When I get up close to it, I see that it has an inscription: *Thank You NHS & Key Workers*. This is a bench to mark the pandemic. This is a bench to remember the loss of lives in the period of intensity in which people, healthcare workers, frontline workers, put their literal lives at risk for the good of others, to ensure that others lived.

It is the first pandemic memorial I have seen, either to the people who died or to the people who fought to save others. It reminds me of the bench in the cemetery near my daughter's grave where I would sit and wait out lunch breaks. I sit on this memorial bench and admire the view, which is out across the fields to Flixton Island, and then beyond to Star Carr. I take a moment to deliberately remember the NHS staff in the pandemic, picturing in my mind the awful loneliness and fear of that time. I picture the courage it must have taken to face that day after day, putting themselves in the path of danger, shielding others, head to foot in protective gear. The way my nurse friend's face was sore and marked by it. And I remember all the farm workers and the cottagers and poor people who lost their connection to the land through the land enclosures, whose voices were not even as much as scratches in the margins of the records. And back to the Star Carr folk and the Palaeolithic people of Flixton Island, and to my dad, and my daughter. They all seem to float to this place where I am, attached to me in this moment of deliberate remembrance. I carry them around with me for a while before touching down into my own life again.

When I turn round and start making my way back along the lane, heading south, I am met by a view I was not expecting. The sides of the valley are imposing. They rise like a wall, a shelf of chalk and field, and I suddenly feel very small in the middle of the lake, very insignificant. The mist is rolling down, the sound has dulled. I am far away from myself again. But as I move back along the lane and the road, I feel myself emerging, rising from the lake to the familiar view that I know, the village and my modern life. I get into my car and switch the heating on, demist the windows, take off my gloves and turn the car around in a little passing place, leaving behind the farmland, returning as the light is fading to my little house, the lamplight in my scruffy office, the sound of the wind in the trees.

# CHAPTER SIX

# The Family Farm

My paternal grandad was a tenant farmer. He did not own the farm that he managed – the farm and the farmhouse in which he brought up his family were owned by someone else. My grandad was one of a long line of tenant farmers, and both my maternal and paternal grandads had connections to horses. My grandad on my mum's side once rescued a stable full of thoroughbred horses during a terrible flood in Thirsk, leading them to safety through the raging waters. My grandad on my dad's side, the farming side, was a small man, five foot four, and the oldest son. The pressure on him as the oldest, to go out and find work and help pay the bills, must have been immense. My dad always said that my grandad struggled to prove himself as a farm labourer because of his size. You need height and heft to throw a bale of hay up and onto a travelling cart at harvest time. But the way I understand it is that he did the work, he pushed himself harder to keep up, to provide for his family and, what's more, he had an affinity with horses. He grew a reputation for being good with horses, and he kept proving himself as a farmer, until he was taken on as a tenant farmer, moving between several farms before settling in the one his father had farmed, and his father's father had farmed.

When I think about roots, I think about the farm. The farm is what I consider to be our ancestral place. It is not in the valley, it is not at the lake. It is westwards, inland, over the Hambleton Hills in Sowerby. My link to the place, to the bricks and mortar of the farmhouse, is fine as a thread, perhaps not there at all. It is a place I am barely sure that I remember. It is the farm my dad and his sisters grew up on. I wish I knew more about it. Since my dad's death the whole of that section of my identity has become unstable. I have a sudden longing to talk to my dad about it, to explore how he felt about his life there. I can't ever ask him about that moment when his own father advised him not to go into farming, and how he felt when he didn't, choosing a different life entirely. I can't ask him anything. And the farm is a long way away, and it is not our farm, we were never the owners.

One day, while researching, I come across a picture of the 'family farm' on the internet. I have to check twice to make sure it is what I think it is. The photograph has been taken in the middle of winter, the field ruts are frosted, and a great bare oak tree is standing in the foreground. In the picture is a sturdy house with six windows and a door on the façade, like a child's drawing of a house. It has a red roof and warm orange bricks that I feel like I remember from my childhood.

The farm is in Sowerby, near Thirsk, about an hour's

drive away from where I live now. I can't remember the last time I was there, but it must have been when I was little, maybe seven years old. My mum insists I would have been too little to remember it. It's the farm that my dad was born in, the farm where his four sisters were born also. It is the farm he grew up in and the farm that his own father, my grandfather, and my great grandfather were attached to as tenant farmers and farm managers. It is an intrinsic part of my family narrative, my family identity. But my family never owned it. It belonged to the farmer whose lands my grandfather farmed and managed. It is ours, and it is not ours.

Once again, I find myself in a strange hinterland, a space in which my ancestors belong, they know the land intimately, but they have no rights to the place. Our oldest family photos are of ancestors sitting in buttoned-up suits and whalebone-corseted dresses outside the farmhouse door. My sister remembers fetching eggs from the chickens and the childhood indignity of being told a hen wouldn't peck her, only to be pecked forcefully by a broody red hen. My brother and sister both remember the rocking horse in the attic; an old dappled white horse with a blond mane, one of those wooden rocking horses mounted on a solid block with a sliding mechanism. I find a picture of it among my auntie Mary's photograph collection. In the photo it is clearly summer, and the horse has been brought out into the garden to be played with. My auntie Norah squints into the sun. She is in a flowery bathing suit and looks about nine or ten. She is holding the harness of the horse, as if about to lead it to Thirsk racetrack. My auntie Mary is mounted on the horse and is saying something to my auntie Rita who is sitting sucking her thumb next to the family dog. In the background, a trellis fence is supporting roses, and behind that are the solid bricks of the farmhouse, which I know are orange even though the photograph is black and white.

My grandparents left the farm in the 1980s. As a child I had assumed that they had some sort of ownership of it and had sold it to buy their little bungalow. But that wasn't the case. My grandparents had saved, and saved hard, to ensure that they would not be destitute when the time came for retirement. When I look at the retirement age now, and the push that our current government is making towards an even later retirement age, and the way that working-class people, who are more likely than any other class to have manual or service jobs, are lumped into a wider group of similar-aged people who may have had jobs that were kinder to joints and muscles, it speaks to me about representation of working-class people, both in positions of power and in the minds of a government primarily made up of middle-, upper-middle- and upper-class people. I feel that it is verging on the impossible to understand what being a builder or a labourer or a cleaner will have done to a person's body by retirement age if you haven't been around those people, except in the background, emptying your bins and cleaning your toilets. That there are so few people from working-class backgrounds within government means that they are simply not considered or rather that they are not understood. When the government pushes for people to work into their seventies, they have in mind people who work in offices, perhaps, an entirely different type of work that is much less punishing to the physical body. Working-class people generally have shorter life spans and one of the reasons is the type of work they tend to do. No one who has been a farm labourer or a builder or a trawlerman would think that a person could work up to and past their sixty-eighth birthday. My own dad, who'd been a bus driver most of his life, but also a builder's labourer at times, retired at sixty-five, having saved enough to retire slightly earlier. He was dead by seventy-one. He got six years. Six years of the retirement he had worked so hard for all his life.

As I write about landscape and livelihood, the enclosure act and the slow degradation of the rights of common people, peasants and the working class to live on the land of their ancestors, I realize I am retelling some of my dad's stories. I am a vehicle for his memories, and now he's gone I can't fact check them. When he was diagnosed with stomach cancer and set out on a journey of intense chemotherapy in Castle Hill Hospital in Hull, I would accompany him on the journey, sometimes with Mum, sometimes just myself and him. All the time that he was ill it felt like he was enduring some terrible rite of passage, a journey into an unknown land that none of us could really accompany him on. All we could do, from our safe place on the other side of his experience, where we were *not* facing death, was offer those practical supports – driving him places, cooking for him.

When we drove to hospital, over the Wolds, over those enormous chalky landscapes, dipping into the villages, travelling along the lines of the Gypsey Race, the winterbourne stream that runs from the Wolds to Bridlington seafront, through places whose names held their Viking and Saxon ancestry, he would tell me about his childhood. We never talked about the cancer, or about recovery or about death, but he was wandering through his life, picking up the parts that meant something to him.

He talked about his dad quite a bit and about the farm. The farm sounded as if it was a precious, almost sacred site, and it felt like that nostalgia for the place was an important part of this journey for my dad, that it might have been important to revisit. Of the plans we made, this was one of them, that while he was recovering after the very serious, very high-risk operation, when he was able to sit in a car seat again, we would drive out and revisit the farm. Then he could tell me the stories of his youth and I would drive him around to visit his childhood haunts. As it happened there was no recovery. There were complications during the surgery, and despite several more high-risk surgeries, one on top of another to fix what had gone wrong, he never came out of the induced coma. After his death, I was left with a half conversation. I felt like I was stepping through a landscape unfamiliar to me, without a guide. When I come across the photograph of the farm I feel, again, a pull to go to visit the place.

My intention is to go alone, to drive there one day and maybe take a picnic and a notebook. To record the landscape and allow my emotions to settle into it, to build up the layers needed to understand my place in this story. In the end, it feels too hard to go somewhere unfamiliar on my own and to risk getting the wrong farmhouse. I abandon my plan for an emotional solo trip and must resort to asking my mum, and then Auntie Mary, my dad's sister, to help. Auntie Mary has not been to the farm for years and is happy to accompany us.

We arrive at the farm in Mary's fabulous little sporty car. Mary has always been a favourite of nieces and nephews. She has a warm face, a sort of lovely shadow of my grandmother's, and in every photo I have seen of her as a child, she looks like a child from a Victorian chocolate advert. She has a kind soul but will take no nonsense. The turn onto the farm track is right on the corner of a surprisingly busy road, the place where the children of the family would catch the bus into Thirsk for school. The way my dad always told it was that he walked miles to school and back, through blizzards and snowdrifts, like an Arctic explorer. I start to see a pattern of a slightly unreliable narrator in his stories.

We wind along the raised, chalky track and suddenly there it is. The farmhouse. And it is much changed from all the photographs and all the imagined stories that I have. Everything I know of it vanishes immediately, and part of me wishes I had not made this journey because the farm I had in my head was much prettier to look at. But I check myself. The farm is like a person. Or like a piece of the landscape. It is very old, hundreds of years old, and has seen so many alterations over those years that it is simply not the place it was when it was built.

My dad was sketchy about the history of the building but was adamant that it had been a leprosy hospital, and that that had been its purpose when it was built. In my research I find that there was a spital nearby, a place for taking care of travellers and the sick, and it's possible the farm was built on that site. One of my aunts tells a tale of the house being haunted: a blocked doorway in one of the upstairs bedrooms, a ghost that rattled the latch of the ancient doors to get access to it, my aunt who would simply leave the door open at night so as not to have her sleep disturbed.

When we step out of the car, I can see the history in the house. At some point since the family left, the house has been split in two. It is now two separate properties. The back of the house is an utter patchwork of different bricks, marking the places where windows and doors had previously been. There are doors gone, new doors in new places, new windows, windows bricked up. Some of these bricked-up scars are obviously very old – I can see the curve of an arched window, a doorway.

The side of the house we are facing is unoccupied, available to rent and awaiting a tenant. The other side is occupied, so we dare not poke about too much. Later, I'll look at pictures of the interior on the estate agency website and be surprised by the low ceilings but wide, deep rooms. The fold yard – a kind of courtyard created by long, red roofed barns forming a square at the back of the farm – is gone, and in its place are industrial barn units in steely greys and hard-wearing metals. The garden is much changed. There are no roses, and it seems smaller than the photographs I have of it. The landscape feels bordered, by telephone wires and railway tracks and roads. It is bleak and plain.

As a child, on one memorable Christmas morning, I woke to find that my dad, with my mum's help, had built me a farm playset, with a green baize grass surface and papier-mâché hedgerows. There was a pond with ducks, a barn with cows and sheep, a tractor with a trailer that dropped plastic bales when pushed forwards. There was a little farmer and a little farmer's wife. When I first found out my dad had this terrible cancer growing in him, my mind went straight to that farm set, and the effort and time that he had put into it, all while working twelve-hour shifts driving buses. It summed him up in so many ways. I look at the family farmhouse now and it reminds me of that playset; it feels like all the elements have been stripped away around it, leaving just a building.

I wander down the farm track towards the next farm on the road. The middle farm, which is no longer a farm, and is now a private house, was recently valued at three million pounds. It is very luxurious and so very different to the family farm with its industrial units and practical, farm labourer cottages. I turn to look at 'our' farm from a different angle, the angle that one of the photos I own, from the 1970s, is taken from. I can see that from the front, from this distance, it *is* recognizable. I can see the farm as it was. It doesn't stir anything in me – I don't remember it. I have a vague memory of my brother and sister and me walking this road and them running off, and the awful anxiety when I couldn't remember which farm was 'ours', but that could be a false memory, a reflection of the guilt I feel in the pit of my stomach because I *want* to feel something. I want to feel something for my dad, to be able to say, '*Yes, here it is, Dad, I can see all your stories now.*' But there isn't anything like that.

We stroll around the farm lanes and up to the little reservoir where two swans are swimming. This is where my grandad's ashes were scattered. It's pretty, peaceful and it's practical – a reservoir for use by farmers. There is a shush of the wind in the trees and the constant alarm calls of pheasants nearby and far away. An owl pellet is on the ground under a beech. I poke it with a stick, but it doesn't yield anything interesting. Nearby, the hum of the electricity pylons is a constant, slightly threatening noise, and the Thirsk bypass, just visible, and the occasional train rumbling past mean it isn't as peaceful as I imagine it would have been when my dad lived here. There are few hedgerows, no pond, no orchard, no chickens, no life, just a bland patchwork of fields. I am romanticizing the past, I think, but still feel a little deflated.

If my dad was here, I think he would bring it to life. Auntie Mary points out her bedroom window. We talk about how they were all born in the house, the slightly mundane experience of being told at school that they suddenly had a sibling, arriving home to an entirely new person in the house, a sudden expansion of family. I take a few photos.

When we drive over to see the third farm on the track, there are people walking by the little beck and I have a memory of us, our family of five, by the beckside, but not here, over towards where my grandad and nana moved to. I realize now that a lot of what we did as children, a lot of the activities that my dad planned for us – the rides out to the moors, the travelling around looking at rundown houses and imagining living there, paddling in becks and camping in deep dark valleys – was him recreating his own youth for us, so that we might enjoy the freedom of a farm lad's life. The smallholding, that Dad worked so hard for, that he worked so hard to *own*, that too was a small-scale recreation of this farm life, a life that his own father gave to him, passing down the joy of the outdoors. Now I carry that joy too.

I look at the skyline behind the farm and see that it is not dissimilar to the valley walls that I see when I step out of my front door. The valley that I have always seen when I have stepped out of my front door. It gives me a sense of home, even though I have never lived here. I think it is the knowledge of the connection, of the land itself, of the love of it. It brings me peace to think that way. As we drive away, I don't feel like looking back. It doesn't really own a place in my heart, and I'm surprised by that. Perhaps, like some sort of chemical catalyst, my dad needed to be attached to it in some way to evoke a feeling, and I don't really feel him there.

# CHAPTER SEVEN

# Folkton

It's April when I come to Folkton. April is the month of the anniversary of my daughter's birth and of her death. I have this on my mind as I park the car and walk down the slope of Folkton village main street, past a huge and newly green willow. I want to turn my face to the sun like a child, to absorb the early spring warmth. The wind is moving through the willow like a wave.

There are lots of very old-looking houses and converted barns and just the one long road which winds down and then turns onto the carr. There is an old red phone box that has been repurposed as an information centre for the village, and then there is the church: typically Norman in style, with a square tower and ivy climbing up the walls.

I'm here to visit the church graveyard and the church itself if it's open. The metal gates are the colour of the 1940s; that dark, jungle green that I equate with old farm doors and enormous enamel tea pots in church halls. The gates are stiff. Initially I think them locked and search for a padlock, but with a good shove I get them open and enter, walking down the sunken path, the headstones at head level, like being led through the underworld. The church is locked, the handle swings round and round uselessly in my hand.

It's a shame, as I've read there's a Romanesque carving of a hare inside. It's thought that Folkton was in fact a Roman military settlement hundreds of years ago. Though whether this hare was a repurposed Roman carving, I do not know. When I read about the hare in this church, I wanted to visit and pay some sort of homage to it. Hares are symbolic of life, fertility, worldliness and magic, and when my daughter died, and I began writing about her, the hare became a symbol for her too.

The first poem I wrote about the experience of pregnancy, that incredible transformative process, used the hare as a metaphor. I wrote about a witch-hare – a witch who can transform into the shape of a hare. I wrote about the feeling of another creature pushing through the body, the growth of it, the delicacy of it, the hare as the ultimate version of wilderness and of wildness.

When I think about my pregnancy, I think in terms of a kind of animal instinct that my body expressed of its own accord. I was compelled to try to capture that in poetry, in prose, in any artform I could for years after her death. It was as if I might bring her back if I could just conjure the exact feeling of my body and hers living and breathing in the same space. When we chose the inscription on her headstone, it too was a poem I had written, a last letter to her. When I wrote my poetry collection, *When I Think of My Body as a Horse*, the hare symbol ran right through it, with the narrator emerging from the hare's body to survive. I wanted to capture our story and pin it down, but it was more than that. The process of writing about her, of using those symbols to capture her, was almost involuntary, a purge, a compulsion. Now, thirteen years later, almost to the day, that compulsion is quenched. Except, here I am again, revisiting in a different way the things that hold us, pin us, remind us.

I vow to return when the church is open so I can see the hare stone carving, but today I will wander around the pretty cemetery. As I pass the wall of the neighbouring farm, I accidentally set their dog to barking. It continues to bark the whole time I am visiting. The sharp sound ricochets off the chalk buildings and I feel suddenly self-conscious, aware that people will be looking to see who is wandering in this tiny place.

It is the first warm day of the year. All around in the villages and the towns the tourists are arriving to make the most of a sunny spring weekend. This village, though, and the churchyard, is mostly peaceful. There is no reason to visit here, unless you are here for a specific purpose, as I am.

The blackthorn is in blossom and small white petals are drifting over the slumped headstones. Blackthorn is one of those plants that feels magical. The wood from a blackthorn is slow-burning, and the leaves can be steeped to make a tea. A witch's wand could be made from a blackthorn, and the deep purple sloe berries have been used to make herbal drinks and sloe gin, or they can be eaten raw after the first frost of the year has sweetened them. Ötzi the Iceman, a frozen mummy from 3350 BC, found defrosting on the border between Austria and Italy in 1991, had sloe berries with him. I am thinking again of the Star Carr people, gathering sloes to eat in the autumn, and the nineteenth-century farming folk from Flixton gathering berries from the hedges on the common land. I'm thinking of this blackthorn hedge in this cemetery and the sloes that will come and how someone, surely, will gather them for gin, because I will do the same in my own village. I was told once that blackthorn trees are a Bronze Age boundary marker. If you see blackthorn in hedges, it's possible that the tree has been there since the Bronze Age, delineating land borders, or acting as a pen for cattle, the hard spikes a deterrent against animals pushing through hedges and escaping. I like the idea of continuity through nature, that the creamy petals drifting over me might have drifted over this land long before me, may have drifted over the lake when it was water, before it was even fenland.

I turn to the north, and I can see Seamer Beacon on the opposite horizon, always the waymarker. I think of my daughter buried all the way over there, on the other side of the valley, below the beacon. Behind the church cemetery, the stubs of well-maintained fruit trees are beginning to blossom. From my spot in the graveyard, I can see three farms and know of another two on the way out of the village. This place is a real mix of the agricultural living village and something more romantic. A couple of the houses have been renovated to a high-end *Country Living* beauty. The others look like they've always looked – white chalk bordered with red brick. The air is full of the calls of crows, blackbirds and chaffinches and jackdaws. Saturday mornings used to be about hangover recovery – from getting hammered in the nightclubs of Scarborough – but now they are about deciphering tithe documents and wandering cemeteries to match names to people I've read about on census forms. I do not miss the hangovers.

It looks like no one has been buried in this churchyard for a long time. The cemetery is mainly filled with headstones from the late 1700s up to the early 1900s. There are a couple that look even older, but I can't read their dates. On some of the headstones the writing has bloomed with age, the lettering weathered. It is as though the words have been lost to the wind, that last tribute from the people who buried their loved ones has been blown away.

Recently I have been deep diving through the online census records to find out who the people of Folkton and Flixton, these two villages so close to each other on the edge of the lake, were. Now, walking round the graveyard, I find myself recognizing the names of individuals, knowing their professions. Few headstones have the occupations of the dead written on them, but one of them proudly states 'blacksmith'. Knowledge of the merest details of these people's lives, lived two hundred years ago, feels one step away from putting names to faces. It feels not dissimilar to walking into a room full of people you vaguely know, albeit they are all silent and made of stone.

There is a single war grave in this cemetery, set back from the other graves and noticeable for its neatness, the sand-coloured stone carefully incised with the French horn and Yorkshire rose emblem of the Yorkshire Light Infantry.

'T. Ireland King's Own Yorkshire LI.'
9th September 1918 aged 37.

This man died just nine weeks before the end of the First World War. A little digging about in census records shows he died at the Western Front, but I don't know the specifics. Later I trace his family backwards through the census, and I see his father, William Ireland, a farm labourer, moving between Flixton and Folkton, working into his late fifties. I learn that Tom Ireland, the man killed in the First World War, was, according to the census in 1911, 'travelling the

Wolds handling machines'. I'm not sure how to interpret this. It's possible I'm misreading the slanty, hastily written description. But it could also be someone with no job title, travelling across the Wolds doing odd jobs, and perhaps this was something he had a skill with, working and maintaining farm machinery. If he had apprenticed at his father's side, it's probably just that. My dad did the same at his father's side, learning to fix tractors, learning to drive farm machinery, how to patch up fences, how to repair boilers and engines of all kinds. While my grandad seems to have had an affinity with horses, my dad had something of an affinity with *horsepower* and could fix pretty much any vehicle, a bonus if you were a bus driver out on a 'magical mystery tour' in the middle of the moors when your bus broke down.

On the anniversary of my daughter's death, I am feeling the familiar, yearly panic about her being forgotten. My pilgrimage to selfhood, to rootedness and belonging, is weighed down today by a desire to know that the dead are not forgotten. It is as if I am trying to find safe harbour for us both, my daughter and me, a place for our memories, as if by anchoring myself somewhere we will be permanent, we will become a part of the archive of the landscape. I am looking for that sense of permanence when I go searching through the census. I worry a lot that the responsibility of her whole life is with me, that there is only my husband and me to remember my daughter. While I am alive, she is physically present in me.

When a woman is pregnant, she exchanges cells with her baby, through the placenta. These cells can migrate all around the body, ending up in the brain, the liver, the heart. They can still be present decades after the birth of the child. It pleases me to be carrying tiny parts of her physical body around in my heart and it saddens me that when I die, I shall be taking her with me.

I have come to this churchyard to acknowledge and honour my landscape ancestors. Perhaps by remembering them I am harbouring their memories like cells. Perhaps when you read this book you will be taking these memories into you too, becoming a part of the story of this place. There is so little of the rural working-class people recorded, so little of their joy, their suffering. But I find them listed in the censuses, and from the censuses I can build pictures of their lives.

Once this pilgrimage is complete, I might find that being remembered doesn't actually matter; that the point isn't to be remembered, it is simply to experience life. What matters is that my daughter lived, that she was real, small but impossibly powerful, with a gravitational pull that caused me to orbit around her. I'm thinking of a poem by a writer friend, John Foggin, who died recently. The poem, from his last collection, *Pressed for Time*, is titled 'In the Meantime'. He used the words of the Venerable Bede to explore his own quick ember of life. Bede wrote, 'the life of man on earth is like the swift flight of a single sparrow through the banqueting hall'. John's poem saw the bird fly through a mead hall, experiencing the bad smells and raucous noise, but also the sound of a harp, and an epic poem in a language it couldn't understand before it disappeared into the night and 'who knows what happens next'.

Just because a life is short it doesn't mean it is meaningless. I think about the sparrow in the mead hall, the brief brightness and smells it experienced. I'm thinking about the women who have lost babies, and the babies who have lost their tiny lives. In the 1911 census, when records were becoming more detailed, there is a section for the number of live births and child deaths a person has experienced. This, I suppose, is an indication of the high infant mortality rates at the time. The number of live births recorded for Sarah Ireland, Tom the soldier's mother, is four, with the number of deceased children recorded as one. After some searching, I find all of Sarah's children – Shushanna, Tom, Walter and Lizzie.

Shushanna (a name related to 'Susan' or 'Susanna') seems to have worked in domestic service. I find a Susanna with the same birth date and same parental names living in Hunmanby in the 1901 census, aged seventeen. She is working as a servant. Hunmanby is just over the ridge of the valley, in walkable distance, though a tough walk up a very steep hill.

Sarah's son, Walter, is ten months old in 1881. That's the only census he appears in. Lizzie Ireland is five years old in the 1891 census. One of Sarah Ireland's children died in infancy. Walter, I think. I search for Walter in the cemetery, but I don't find him. Maybe he is one of the spaces between headstones in which the poorest people are buried.

Tom's name is on the war memorial situated between the two villages. There are other names on the memorial too, but those boys are not buried in this cemetery. Perhaps they are in some corner of a foreign field that is forever England. Who knows. Even this, after all this time, is shocking, the waste of these young lives. Tom, not so young at thirty-seven. Shocking that they died, shocking that families lost their providers, shocking that this man never seemed to quite land on his feet, that this would be his end. The war memorial is well maintained, bedecked with flowers and a little fence. The two world wars are on two sides of the stone memorial, another two sides are left blank, awaiting the next set of names, the next world war.

Between these two tiny villages, war came and took eight young men, including Tom.

There is a temptation to go home and set about continuing these narratives; finding out exactly what happened to the people laid to rest in this graveyard. I don't know why I am drawn to these strangers' stories; these are not *my people*; this is not *my* story. Except, in a way, all the people living in this valley are my people, all the people walking this land are my people. I inevitably have some shared human experiences with these long-ago folk. But the thing that really joins us is the landscape. They too walked under this ridge of the Wolds, they too watched the blackthorn blossoms float on the wind, heard the crows and blackbirds in the trees, the 'snooker balls on the break' call of the jackdaws.

Margaret Atwood in her book *Negotiating with the Dead* said that '. . . all writing of the narrative kind, and perhaps all writing, is motivated, deep down, by a fear of mortality – by a desire to make the risky trip to the Underworld, and to bring someone back from the dead'. I have spent so long trying to bring my daughter back from the dead. I am aware that by writing poetry collections about my daughter I have been crossing into and out of the Underworld for years, but there is also something more to the journey. I am attempting to bring myself back from that place, the place I went all those years ago when I began to forsake my authentic self. Today I make a point of placing myself in the moment. I make a point of standing still in the warm sunshine and spending a couple of minutes paying my respects, as the scent of cut grass wafts from the orchard next door where someone is driving a mower around the trees. I especially make a point of remembering and acknowledging Sarah Ireland.

I stand quietly and feel for the archive of the landscape, place myself in its record and think – *You are remembered.* I make a point of existing in the moment and recognizing the shared experience of loss, the animal instincts of the human body in pregnancy, in motherhood, in grief. The deaths of her two children – little Walter at some point, and then Tom, shot and killed in the First World War – are so very, very different to my own loss, and yet I imagine Sarah in the midst of grief, in the village I've walked through, in a house on North Street that I think I've passed, in the kitchen, in the bedroom, at the window, in the garden, grieving but carrying on, and I *know* it. I imagine Sarah and William standing at the war memorial, seeing the bright white of their son's name newly etched into the stone. I imagine them leaving this place. Perhaps too many memories weighing them down to stay here.

On the anniversary of my daughter's birthday, the anniversary of her death, I take flowers to her grave. I bring a dinosaur-shaped planter, pink roses and the gorgeous bouquet sent from my mother-in-law. By the time I get there my own mum has already been, leaving three pots of grape hyacinths. I post a poem on my blog in remembrance of my daughter, write a short passage repeating her story for any new followers, then make the decision to step away.

I am going on another pilgrimage today. My intention is to find the site of a Neolithic child burial and an interesting archaeological artefact, the Folkton Drums. I feel on firmer ground. While I find the concept of belonging and my need to fit in – or rather my need to find belonging

in a way that feels right for me, the *authentic* me – difficult
to put into words and practice, there is one place where I
have seen my experience mirrored. It is not the specific
circumstances of baby loss, child loss or miscarriage that
connect grieving mothers – after all, every experience is
different – but I feel the *instincts* around that experience
are similar. I am setting out to find the place in which a
Neolithic family, maybe a Neolithic village, came to lay
their children to rest. I want to see myself in the people
who came before me. I know that when I search like this,
I am not really searching for them, I am searching for
myself in them, a kind of shared experience. It is more
than just wanting to pay my respects at a place where
someone buried their child, but there is that too. I want
to stand at the place where my ancestors stood in front of
this child's grave and say, 'I'm here. We're still doing this.
I did this too.'

The Folkton Drums are grave goods found within a
Neolithic child burial site on Folkton Wold, just above the
village of Folkton. I have always been fascinated by them.
They are an archaeological mystery – no one knows what
they were used for. The Folkton Drums are three cylin-
drical chalk objects of graduating size, not actual drums
at all, just vaguely drum-shaped. They are small enough
to be portable, the largest is about the size of a large coffee
mug. They are decorated on the sides and on the tops, but
not the bases. The decorations are typical of Neolithic art
– geometric patterns, dots and lines, triangles, diamonds
and shapes that vaguely resemble eyes and eyebrows. On
this pilgrimage I want to find the burial place of the child
in whose grave the drums were left.

I park again outside the cemetery at Folkton and go
looking for a public footpath that will take me up and out

of the valley. The public footpath sign points straight into a hedge, and I can't find a way through, so I double back on myself to what I think is a private road leading up to some holiday cottages and a sawmill. I give it a try anyway, feeling that flip-flap of anxiety as I venture into the unknown. I see, almost immediately, that there is a place for people to leave their dog poo bags, so at the very least it looks like people – people who dispose of their dog's waste at least – must be tolerated on the private road.

The road is steep and shaded with tree dapple. The smell of sawdust is everywhere, and then the smell of farming. I am climbing up the side of the valley. It is physically challenging to get out. Growing up it felt psychologically difficult too, as if the valley walls were a metaphor for the hard work it would take to get away from home and study at university or leave for other towns or cities. For the hard work it would take to push back against my own anxiety, against the expectations of society, against all the doubt and imposter syndrome that came with choosing a different life. I have three degrees: a biomedical science degree funded by the hospital I worked for, a BA in English literature from the Open University and an MA in creative writing. I completed my BA and MA through distance learning. After I had finished these degrees, I thought I might like to prove myself and do a part-time PhD at Hull University. I applied and, much to my surprise, I was awarded a fee-paying place, just missing out on a scholarship. I was excited about the university experience, the *real* university experience, not the one that I'd experienced from my kitchen table, or on day release. I had missed out on having the real university experience because I left school at sixteen and went straight into work.

I imagined my PhD student self as a confident, intelligent

woman walking the corridors, researching in the grand library, talking expressively at podiums, at conferences. In my mind, a little montage of this confident woman would play out – here she is, almost asleep over a pile of books in the library, studying by lamplight as the cleaners hoover in the background. Here she is in a seminar room, passionately conveying her points about nineteenth-century English literature. Here she is running across campus late for a lecture, and here having drinks with other confident PhD students. And here, look, her parents wiping a tear away, her husband with a great big bunch of flowers, while this slim, attractive, confident woman walks across the stage in a floppy hat, receiving her scroll, her PhD. I have no idea who that woman was. But it wasn't me. How many years did it take me to realize that the composite of smart, intelligent, beautiful women that I had tried to wriggle myself into wasn't me? I thought university would make me the kind of person who could fit in, but the reality was so different.

On one of the first days at university, when I was supposed to attend a sort of mixer occasion and meet the other PhD students, I sat in my car and cried because my anxiety was so severe I didn't know if I would be able to enter the building. I'd got lost on campus and then fled back to my car like the coward I felt I was. When I finally made it in there, everyone seemed to know each other already. I didn't know how to broach the silence. I didn't know how to make conversation. I began to wither.

Once I got started with my research, I felt overwhelmed, aware that I was working a full-time job at minimum wage to pay the fees and then not being able to find enough time for the coursework. My supervisor was changed because the department was shuffling roles, and it unsettled me. Every time I thought I'd found my feet, something else happened that made me doubt myself. It bled into the work I was trying to produce. I couldn't write well. I couldn't find my way into the subject. My nightmares, all of them, were coming true. My default reaction was to think of myself as stupid for even trying. *Who did you think you were? This is not for you.* The drumbeat that lived in my head projected onto everything. I don't know where I thought my anxiety would go when I went to university. The woman in my montage didn't have anxiety, she was simply living her best life, in my head somewhere, while I was sitting in my car, again, crying.

My experience of university was not social drinks after seminars or studying until late in the library, putting the hours in and enjoying the intensity of learning. My experience was one of slowly being ground down and being too embarrassed to ask for help, not knowing what it was I'd be asking for anyway, because at the time I thought that I was broken, embarrassingly broken and unfixable, and that if I was any sort of scholar, I would just pull myself together and get on with it. I felt out of place, my accent stood out, my questions were stupid, I wasn't 'passing' as a PhD student. I was struggling financially, and while the people I approached for help with funding tried their best, they were, I think, used to dealing with students who perhaps had more money or some funding because their suggestions were to take on extra work. My main work, my minimum wage job, was already full time. I'd made a terrible mistake. I'd thought that I would manage financially. But I just couldn't earn enough and on top of this I had the utterly exhausting anxiety and imposter syndrome.

Every time I drove up the winding road and out of the

valley on my way across the Wolds to university, it felt like I was struggling to get out of the dark valley bottom, like an animal trying to escape a trap. The day I decided to pack it in, thousands of pounds down and with nothing to show for it but the heavy weight of depression and a complete burnout, I drove back through the sunlit wheat fields, opened my windows, and laughed and cried into the scent of oilseed rape. I felt like I had removed a horrible, itchy mask and was throwing it out of the car window. I drove down the steep winding track and returned to my roots, where I felt I belonged. I pulled the car over on the carrland and got out, and I stood on the little bridge and breathed in, great gulping breaths of the green landscape, and I felt better. I recovered.

This sort of thing happens all the time to lots of people. I don't think I realized how often it happens until I posted on social media about how shit I felt walking away. When I made that tweet and people began responding, I saw that there were many people who had had similar experiences. People who had a non-traditional route into university, distance learners, working-class people, people from ethnic minority backgrounds, autistic people, people who had anxiety, people with physical disabilities, people who re- alized that it wasn't for them, that they just couldn't fit in. They'd all walked away too. It's so hard to break away and do something like this, to climb out of the place you were born and exist in a world that isn't really built for you. I still feel the sting of it, the shame of it, but less so now. I found a different route to what I wanted to do and am happy here. I do think I would have looked good in that floppy hat though.

143

I break out into the strong sunshine and turn to see how far up I am. The view is beginning to expand, but I have so much further to climb until I reach the top of the valley, until I am climbing out of it, away from the lake site, and heading onto the Yorkshire Wolds. All is chalk beneath my feet, and the hillside around me has chalk bones poking through. Here and there are lumps of land which I'm almost sure are tumuli, the prehistoric burial mounds. You can't throw a stick around here without hitting a tumulus, but mostly they are softened, dug out or ploughed down until their shape is mellowed and indistinguishable from the natural landscape.

My heart is bursting out of my chest, and I feel like I can't breathe, but it is exhilarating. It feels so good to push my body back into the shape of the climber, the walker, and out of the comfortable settle of my daytime, deskbound shape. There is a bench on the rise right at this point, and when I get close to it, I see that it is another bench dedicated to the NHS workers. Its sister bench is at the lake edge, near to Flixton Island, all the way down in the dip of the valley. I scan my eyes over the place where it should be, but I can't quite make it out from here. The two are like stars in a constellation, and the lake and the valley are the black sky.

I continue to climb out of the valley, passing a silent, empty farmyard as I round the corner and follow the small yellow public footpath guidance arrows on fence posts around the back of the yard where a small, open-fronted barn full of sheep watches me pass. On the other side of the barn, I see the view down into the valley for the last time as I go over the tops and into the Wolds proper.

What a difference in landscape. Suddenly there are few trees and just a straggle here and there of hawthorn. There is green wheat as far as the eye can see. There are skylarks, so many skylarks, but other birds, other plants, other wildlife are noticeable for their absence. It is beautiful in its own way. It is simple and elegant and the underneath, the structure of the Wolds – all those creases and folds of land, the natural dry valleys – is stunning. But the landscape is so far away from being wild. I am now following the edges of the fields. Later, when I look at this place on Google Earth, I can see a huge patchwork of mostly square fields. When I zoom out further, more fields, and again, more fields. The whole place is fields.

We have always grown wheat on the Wolds. I named the magazine I run *Spelt* because that type of long-lived farming of wheat felt like a symbol of longevity for a magazine focused on the creative expression of the real rural. I'm unsettled despite this. I try to be objective rather than emotional. This is a living landscape; rural people are managing the land they live intimately on. This is an observation, not a criticism. When the country was on its knees at the end of the last war, we needed to feed a lot of people and we needed to do it fast and the drive towards industrial methods of farming ensured that no piece of land was lost that could be farmed.

On those long trips to chemo with my dad, as we drove through the Wolds, he often described the orchard on the farm he grew up on, the ground that was really no use to anyone. He told me how the orchard was pulled out, the hedges too, and how it was all burned down so that the farmer could reclaim that small piece of land for growing crops. My dad told me how it broke his heart and likely broke my grandad's too. But it worked. Along with increased use of pesticides and herbicides, chemical fertilization schemes and increased factory farming of animals, food production increased. But now it feels like we are paying the piper. The food has become devalued, the work of farmers, labourers, land managers has become devalued alongside it. We find the consequences of this mass production in the lack of habitat for our native wildlife. An empty sky, no insects, death in the beehives. I feel spoiled to live in the village I do, where each field has a hawthorn hedge, and a protected passage of long grasses where ground-nesting birds exist. Where there are regular copses of trees, where the sightline is broken up by patches of wild ground.

The next part of this pilgrimage to the Neolithic burial site involves me crossing into completely unknown, privately owned territory. On the map, the route passes straight through the middle of a farm. I find myself checking and checking again that I am in the correct place. I do not want to trespass; I do not want to bother the farmer. I make sure, when I see, in the distance, a car crawling away up the long, long drive from the farmhouse itself, that I have my map out, that I look like a conscientious walker eager not to step on land that isn't mine. I am acutely aware that I am a lone woman walker too, and it makes me nervous. After passing between two enormous barns full of screaming pigs, a sound that briefly terrifies me, I see the gate on the other side and make for it. The relief as the sound of squealing pigs recedes is enormous. I am at the top of Folkton Wold now, and in the distance I can see the great X where four dry valleys meet. I'm nearly at my destination.

As I'm making my way along the edge of the field, I can see a labourer in a tractor, dragging ploughing equipment. The field is being turned for planting. They are planting potatoes round and about me. I don't want to be in anyone's way, and again I'm aware that I'm a lone woman, walking in an isolated area. I see the labourer stop, turn the tractor, and reverse up the hill, blades pointed towards me. I have no idea what his intention is, so I stop and wait to see where he is going. He pulls the blades in front of me and then sits in his cab with his hands behind his head, as if on a break. I can't tell if he has seen me, if this is a joke. I wait patiently, doing the thing that women are trained to do, making myself look unthreatening, avoiding eye contact, not communicating, while internally anxious and aware of the potential dangers involved here.

I know several women walkers, solo walkers like me, who go out on the Wolds and the moors and explore ruins and deserted medieval villages and hidden waterfalls. And we all know that inherent in our solo female walking is a danger to our personal safety. My friend was sexually harassed at a well-known beauty spot. A man masturbated openly, directing himself towards her. He exposed himself in an act made to make her feel frightened, uncomfortable, intimidated. She didn't have phone signal and had to do what we, as women, often have to do – ignore it, and hope for the best while walking away, knowing full well that we are vulnerable. She refuses to be cowed by the experience and I'm glad, but so angry for her, for us, for our vulnerability, for the fact that women cannot even access this space, that to be a woman and exist in a public space, even a semi-wild space, is to be in the arena of men.

In a 2021 article in the architectural journal *The Developer*, Dr Ammar Azzouz and Professor Pippa Catterall wrote about the difficulties of creating safe spaces for minority groups because 'most public spaces are male spaces'. The article continues, 'It is men that do the looking in such spaces and whose voices carry and dominate their soundscapes, while marginalised groups tend to seek invisibility within these spaces or avoid them altogether.' The article stayed with me because it rang true. How does this apply to the experience of being a woman in a rural environment? There is nothing architectural here, but I might draw parallels to the way that land management is dominated by white, middle-class males. And because the lens through which we view that environment – through nature writing, through television, through journalism – is predominantly a white, middle-class, male experience, it perhaps automatically creates the impression that these environments are for men first and foremost. At this point in my Folkton Wold pilgrimage, I am certainly feeling that sense of not belonging. Even if my perception of the events unfolding before me is wrong, even if this man is completely innocently going about his job, or he doesn't understand in any way that he might be causing me to feel intimidated, my perception of the situation hasn't simply arrived from nowhere. It has arrived through my experience as a woman who has lived her life in rural and semi-rural areas. Once, walking down a local lane with my elderly dog, a man in an enormous four-by-four slewed round the corner and nearly knocked me and my dog down. I was so frightened and unnerved that I shouted at him as he drove away. Minutes later he returned and drove repeatedly up and down the lane, at speed, forcing me onto the verge with my old dog. It was terrifying and yet I wasn't sure whether to report it to the police. I questioned whether anyone would take me seriously, whether my perception was skewed. So many men do not live these experiences and seem to have the opinion that most men are harmless and that women are misinterpreting their lived experiences.

Standing here, in front of the plough blades, waiting to see what happens next, I feel exhausted by it, by the hyper-vigilance, by the necessity to know what might occur, even if it probably won't. Eventually the farmer drives away and resumes ploughing and I continue on, making sure that every now and again I check behind me. I feel I might be giving farmers or farm workers rough treatment here. I should add that I know plenty of farmers, men and women, who are welcoming and lovely and interested in the stewardship of their land, especially if there is a public footpath running through it and especially if there is an interesting history, a tumulus, a long barrow, a cairn on the land.

I stop just before I reach the place I'm heading and take a video on my phone. I'm trying to capture the peacefulness. I am facing the Neolithic burial site, where a little child was buried with the Folkton Drums. I think of what it must have been like to be alive during the Neolithic period, when the people of this place were beginning to farm, were beginning to make their mark, were moving through the landscape feeling a sense of ownership, and how this was being explored through the ritual grave goods and the building of henge structures, the stone temples made to align with the solstices.

The sound of the tractor dies away. I think, deliberately, about the child in the grave. When we buried my daughter, we put items into her grave. We were not leaving gifts to be taken into the next life, we were still caught in a need to care for her – that instinct was all-consuming. We left a photo of us and the dog, a letter, a toy cat. In the Neolithic grave: a bone pin, the Folkton Drums.

There are so many theories about the drums and their purpose. Some people believe they were used as a tool for building stone circles and henge sites. The theory is that they are measuring devices, that each drum circumference was a specific measurement and that by winding string around the drums a person could create symmetrical spaces using that measurement. Other people believe they were purely decorative. Some people think they were toys. To me, they look like teaching aids, or a kind of seasonal clock. The winter on one side, the summer on the other, the days narrowing to a point in the cross of the year. It seems to me that the cycles of the seasons move round the drum, a continuous turning. Why three drums in one grave? Why the graduating size? Perhaps they represented different seasons, perhaps they represented different events.

Fifteen miles away, in the village of Burton Agnes, another chalk 'drum' from another child burial was found in 2015. Whereas the Folkton Drums were three 'drums' in a single child burial, aligned along the child's back – the largest behind the child's head, the smallest behind the child's pelvis – the Burton Agnes drum was a single 'drum' in the grave of three children. It was placed behind the head of the oldest, largest child. In front of this child, two other little bairns faced each other holding hands, the older child embracing them.

In a strange thread of the web that is my life, Burton Agnes is a few fields west from the industrial estate where I worked on a production line in a cake factory, the place where I first realized I could live independently from an entirely unsuitable man with whom I lived in Bridlington. And many years ago, when my dad drove buses, he would take day trippers to Burton Agnes Hall and tell them stories of the screaming skull, a head bricked into one of the walls there. Once again, I am reminded that this landscape is a mycorrhizal network of memory to me, that my life is embedded in place, my memories too.

The Burton Agnes drum has a design that is similar to the Folkton Drums, but with differences in artwork. It has similar diamonds and shading on the one side, but on the other an extraordinary swathe of concentric circles like a Van Gogh night sky. Found with a bone pin and a chalk ball, this discovery allowed for the drums to be dated, and thus allowed a better idea of the age of the Folkton Drums, which had previously been difficult to date. I was lucky enough to see all the drums together at the British Museum on my trip down to the 'World of Stonehenge' exhibition, and my breath was taken away. The condition of the Burton Agnes drum is pristine. When I saw them in the quiet reverence of the softly lit exhibition, I felt a strange sense of pride, as if I had anything at all to do with their making, their finding, but perhaps this is about that link again, the mycorrhizal network, the fungal spores of belonging and identity. These beautiful, important things came from my homeland and are a part of me and my story too.

I was moved by the art, the markings on the drums. In some places the design was rough, uneven, not quite as symmetrical as the carver might have liked it, in some places it was perfect. There was something so human about it, about the compulsion to create, capture, express.

This sort of art is similar to other Neolithic art around the UK, from the furthest islands of Scotland, to the furthest south our little island stretches. At some point in the Neolithic period, there seems to have been a surge of visual art, and at the same time an increase in grave goods, houses, structures. In the chain of expression, the drums themselves have inspired contemporary artists to create. Like Rose Ferraby, archaeologist and visual artist, who was commissioned to create art for the British Museum. One of her linocuts, my own personal favourite, depicts a land-scape influenced by the patterns on the Folkton Drums. The star on top of one of the drums is depicted shining brightly above a pod-like grave, and inside the grave a child is foetal, a sleeping skeleton. Rose's artwork accompanies a poem by Michael Rosen. The poem is about grave goods and features the Folkton Drums. I find this tribute particularly moving, knowing Michael himself suffered the death of his son. I wonder where the connection point is in this case – death, loss, art. It feels like the ripples on those concentric circles are pulling us towards each other, art influencing art influencing art. I like that I too am attached here, and I feel a genuine sense of belonging when I think about this network of expression.

Looking around the field, there is nothing to see of the Folkton burial mound. It has long ago been removed or ploughed out. It is marked on older maps. It is simply a slope of the landscape, even the wound of itself healed. But being here feels special anyway. I am taken back to the day I buried my daughter. A day of soft breeze and blossoms. I imagine the little bairn in the ground with the drums at their back. And a family like mine at this grave, as my family stood at my daughter's grave, and then afterwards the people who would build the mound around it, building it carefully with permanence in mind. We only know them through what they left behind: a mound that used to be visible to anyone travelling this way, three mysterious chalk objects. We cannot know the people at all. We cannot even imagine the people who were here. But I can imagine the mother's pain. That pain is unchanged because it is a wild pain, a pain born from instinct.

As I turn towards the path home, something catches my eye in the exposed roots of a hawthorn. It is a fossil, hard chalk, about the size of a fifty-pence piece. It has concentric ridges, a part of a mollusc perhaps. It is much less defined than some of the fossils I own. When I run my thumb over the surface it feels gritty, the ridges are almost striped a sandy brown. This then, another link, the shallow sea that this place was before any humans walked here. It reminds me of the star shapes on the Burton Agnes drum, the concentric circles like light glowing from a central point. I pick up the fossil and put it in my pocket. It shall sit on my desk as I write. Another pilgrim badge to mark my journey.

The Yorkshire Wolds Way and the Centenary Way, both very popular walking routes, stalk off from here and I turn and follow one back up and out of the valley, passing two older women walkers on the way. We chat about the landscape. They ask where I have walked from. I'm local, I say, I came from down in the valley. I've come to see the place where the Folkton Drums were found. I point it out to them, tell them to see it in the British Museum. They've come from Staxton Wold, and they tell me about the paths they've walked that day and how they keep telling their friends to come and walk the Yorkshire Wolds Way, how beautiful it is, but that people don't know it very well, people don't seem to have heard of it as much as other walking routes. They're not from round here, and they can't stay for long. They must make the next stop on the Wolds Way before nightfall, and I don't want to hold them up.

I emerge onto the road and move down the slope towards Folkton village. I am back in the land of hedges and birdsong, and it feels like emerging from an entirely different type of landscape. I'm on my way back down again, back to the village, back to my car, and back and back to a hot shower, the light in my office. My husband returns and we visit the old pub, eat, drink and, later, a glass of wine, a shared remembrance of the time we held our daughter, a million years ago and no time at all.

# CHAPTER EIGHT

# Eastfield

It is mid-May and all around are the bright yellow fields of oilseed rape. The village lanes are thick with plants. Each square foot of verge is crowded with green. Cow parsley, bluebells, campions, garlic mustard, cleavers sticking to everything, a feast for my elderly dog who slow walks and stops often to sniff and eat. The trees are now in leaf, even the beech, even the oak, even the ash, all delicately presenting themselves to the heat of the sun.

So far, this year has been wet. The greening up of the landscape has occurred almost overnight after a few particularly heavy days of rain. When the rain stops, it is like a magic trick: sweeping aside like a curtain to reveal that, where just a couple of days ago there was muddy grass and bare branches, there is now green, green, green.

On the day the swifts return it is the first day this year that I've left the house without a jacket. I am back in my happy place – T-shirt, shorts, walking sandals, dog, road, the endless adventure of seeing nature developing, cycling through life stages. Already I pass head-height hedges and hear baby birds being fed within, already the orange tip butterflies, small whites, peacocks too are drifting and spinning and the swifts, oh, the joy of their return. A familiar screech in the sky above the village then the sudden stream of them overhead. To everyone I meet I say, *The swifts are back*, and we share the excitement.

Today's pilgrimage is a strange one. I want to return to my secondary school and then I want to follow the path of my life, my trail away from the lake site, looking for myself in the cafés and holiday flats and hotels where I learned how to work, how to change myself to be what an employer wanted me to be. How sometimes that was impossible. This, I think, is a pilgrimage of forgiveness and acceptance. First, I want to confront the utter misery of school, return to the school gates and wave at the forlorn ghost of myself, show her where we are now. But before I can do any of that, I need to drive out to see my mum.

I have the windows down and am driving a circuit around the lake site, revelling in the quiet time before the tourist season starts and the roads become near impossible to get through, the towns impossible to park in, walk in, visit, exist in.

I have always enjoyed the idea of people as guests here, that we might share this glorious place, in the same way I feel myself a guest in London, experiencing the museums, the bars, the restaurants, the history. But sometimes it's wearing. In the local 'moan' group on social media, someone, a local, has the audacity to be cross at the number of camper vans parked on the road along the cliff tops. The returning anger from tourists in the group who feel a connection to this place is palpable. *We pay your wages. If it wasn't for us your town would be nothing.* And it's true, to a certain extent. Tourism is the trade of the towns on the coast here. But the towns here are not a theme park. These are living, working places, often with complex fishing and agricultural industries and other non-tourism-related trade.

When I get to my mum's house, she is a bit stressed. She's heading out on holiday in a few days with her sisters. I can't tell how much of this is holiday stress and how much of this is grief stress. It's not even a year since my dad died and every new experience brings an element of guilt, for leaving the home, for leaving without him, for leaving and putting herself first, for even having fun without him. Guilty for smiling, guilt and a terrible sadness about the things he is missing. She is at the stage of grief when there is a breaking away, as if he is still being carried along with her, but she is now having new experiences, ones that don't involve him. It hurts me to watch her struggle with this stage of grief, the letting go stage.

I'm looking after her chickens while she's gone. We've talked recently of scaling down the smallholding, losing some of the enormous veg patch, getting rid of the chickens. It might be too soon yet, but it's good to have the ideas floating about. We agree that we should keep options open. I want her to be happy. I know Dad would want her not to be in a state of worry, but grief is glacial, it moves slowly through a life, reshaping it, grinding the edges off it. It is a slow, slow process. They worked so hard for this place, not just to have a life full of adventures, but to own their own land, to live where no one could come and remove them on a whim.

After I leave my mum, I find myself navigating the lakeside again. I am travelling the ancient trade routes: first to York, then inland to Hunmanby and Filey on the coast, then crossing the land bridge from south to north, then up and eastwards towards Scarborough.

I park up and enjoy a walk through the decaying Victorian grandeur of Scarborough town, revisiting some old haunts. First the holiday flats down the road that my dad once owned, then the hotel where I was employed at fourteen as a kitchen hand, then on to the seafront where I'd worked as a waitress for the shortest amount of time ever. Then up into town to sit in my favourite café, a place that used to be a trading shop selling coffee and tea and all things domestic when Scarborough was in its heyday as a spa town.

People forget, though, that before the rich folk discovered the healing benefits of what mid-seventeenth-century people called the 'spaw', the town had a thriving fishing industry. The people who lived and worked here did so at the edge of the land, bringing fish in to salt and trade. Filey, too, was a fishing town, and up the road Hunmanby was an important place of trade. These are Viking landed towns, or some of them are, at least. It's all a bit murky, history wise, but that doesn't stop people from celebrating their 'Viking ancestry'. Flamborough, just a little way up the coast and known for its white chalk cliffs and its smugglers' coves, takes the Viking heritage quite seriously with a New Year's Eve fire march, everyone dressed up as Vikings.

The café I am sitting in is just around the corner from The Grand Hotel, which sits on the site of the holiday cottages where Anne Brontë died in 1849. Her grave is a ten-minute walk away at St Mary's Church. It's nice to sit and watch the people go by. I enjoy that sense of familiarity, though I'm not here as often as I used to be, preferring the small-town quaintness of Filey. At one time I came here to work, and later I lived here, in a tiny Victorian terrace, the front door opening directly onto the street.

After I've picked up a few bits and bobs from the high street, with its mix of innovative street landscaping and street art alongside boarded-up shops and homeless people sleeping in doorways, I cut back and drive along the northern edge of the lake site, to Eastfield and the secondary school I attended.

I attended secondary school in the nineties. The school I went to was on a council estate but took in children from villages all around the valley. My friend who lived over in Flixton would be brought to school in a taxi as she was not on the bus route and was deemed rural enough for the pick-up service. Most people got the bus, either the subsidized school bus or the local bus that circled around the villages and between the towns. I often walked the two-mile route to school.

In my school there was a mix of lower-working-class, upper-working-class and lower-middle-class kids. Mostly the kids at the school were working class, some on the poverty end of the spectrum. I don't think we had any upper-middle-class kids there, but it's all a bit hazy and a long time ago and perhaps I just wasn't aware of the hierarchy then. After all, class is a strange, slightly malleable thing. It's very difficult to categorize sometimes and causes confusion. What I do know is that it felt like the children in the school were funnelled out to the jobs in the town.

I feel that a lot of what was going on at this time was cultural. *You have to see it to be it.* We did not see it. I was a bright student, but I struggled at school, swinging between being in the very top classes in English and science and the very bottom classes for maths. I later realized – much, much later, in my forties at this strange time of self-reflection – that I probably have dyscalculia, a form of maths and number-based dyslexia. I still tell the time backwards sometimes and read bus timetables wrong, as if the numbers change when I'm not looking. It did not stop me from getting a biomedical science degree. I found, later in my life, that given time I was more than capable of solving complex mathematical equations and molecular diffusions, but I did not come to the solutions in the way that other people seemed to. I still got there though.

At school they didn't know what to do with me because of my maths scores. How could someone second to top in the entire school in English be almost bottom in maths? Unbelievably, at forty-six years old, I am still carrying shame around with me because I wasn't good at maths. My anxiety completely ruled me and made it impossible to do simple things like raise my hand in class. I could navigate the anxiety if I was playing a part – telling jokes or playing the clown – but in maths I didn't seem to be able to do that. I can feel the burning in my cheeks as I am writing this, as if I am standing in maths class and we are still playing the game in which the whole class stood, and then one by one you sat down when you correctly answered a maths question, until everyone had got one correct and everyone was sitting down. I am still the last person standing in that class, my mind completely blank because the anxiety of the situation is stripping away everything in my head except the fact that everyone is looking at me. I would leave classes like this one, and some others physically shaking (French was a particularly brutal class because, once again, there were quick-fire questions in front of other students).

I had serious issues with anxiety at school. I don't know if it was just the way life was in the early nineties, but I never received support for this anxiety. I never asked for support. I was too anxious to ask for support, and I wouldn't have really known what to ask for. At the time I was so utterly convinced that I was broken in some terrible way and to ask for help would mean admitting it. I have read that this is actually very common in autistic children. It's another thing that has pulled me towards seeking diagnosis. No one around me asked for support on my behalf, perhaps not realizing that they *could* ask for support. Or perhaps the people who could have done that just accepted that this was the way I was – a bit odd, very shy. Perhaps they hoped I would simply grow out of it. I have not grown out of it. I cannot grow out of it. It is just who I am.

I was mercilessly bullied, very unpopular and very miserable right through school. My oddness was not something I could change. I could cover it, and God I tried to – losing weight, wearing make-up, agonizing over my hair, my clothes, always getting it wrong as if there was some mysterious set of rules that everyone around me knew but I didn't. Somehow people always sensed that I was different. It was like they could smell it on me. They knew that I was *other*. I was so unpopular, such an oddity, that I was often the butt of practical jokes. These were jokes based around the fact that nobody would ever find me attractive, so they would dare each other to pretend to ask me out or, in one memorable case, to put a hand up my skirt. It sounds so brutal now, looking back. It *was* brutal. I am telling you this, not because I want your pity, but because I want you to see the other girls like me who I have no doubt still exist, and for you to notice them, and perhaps even help them. I am looking at my fourteen- or fifteen-year-old self and I am telling her that it gets better. That one day you will turn around and realize that the thing that made you different, the thing that made you not fit in, is the thing that makes you special. Your brain is a strange thing, but it is an utterly beautiful thing. By the end of school I was ready to leave. I wanted out at sixteen and relished the brief freedom between leaving school and getting an actual job.

There were children at the school who had terrible experiences just because they were poor or because they lived on the council estate near the school. They were simply not expected to do anything except be funnelled through the system into the tourism trade or the factories – the frozen chip factory, the bus-making factory, the printing factories.

There is absolutely nothing wrong with any of those jobs. I did factory work for about seven years, before I decided to try my hand as a lab assistant. But the problem was that it didn't really feel like a choice. My interpretation is that if you came off a council estate the expectation was that you would end up cleaning caravans, serving in a café, working in a tourist tat shop or standing on a production line. At the time, I couldn't see any problem with that, and I didn't think to object to any of it because, again, you have to see it to be it, and the opportunities were not there. Only the gifted kids, or the kids with parents who could afford to have their children tutored and prepped, got to break out of that mould. If you were not from a family who could recognize your skills, your abilities, and if you already had, hanging over you, the stigma of poverty, of growing up on the council estate, you had to fight twice as hard to be noticed, and you could only do that if you recognized that you *should* be fighting, if you realized that there was something to fight against.

I cut my teeth in the tourist trade. My first job was as an unpaid volunteer in the holiday flats that my dad bought when holidays abroad were becoming dirt cheap, cheap enough for working-class folk to afford, meaning many of the British tourist towns were facing financial crisis. My dad saw this as an opportunity. He'd paid off the mortgage on the house we grew up in, so he could then get a new mortgage on a block of holiday flats.

The building was on a street leading towards North Bay. You could smell the sea, always. It was a tall, sandy-coloured Victorian terrace, and the house had an attic, a first floor and a ground floor. Four flats in all, with a shared toilet and a shared bathroom. My dad worked full time as a bus driver and repaired, painted, decorated, maintained and cleaned the flats after work and on weekends. I remember this time, when I was about nine or ten, as being a time when I so rarely saw my dad, how he would get in after dark, eat a dinner warmed up by my mum, then fall asleep in the chair. Then get up to go and drive buses all day before heading to the flats to fix the plumbing and paint the hallways. One of the photos we used on the funeral order of service showed him up a ladder, roller in hand, little blue cap and paint-stained jacket on, doing the hallway woodchip of the flats in eggshell. The little blue cap, flecked with paint, is on a chair in the hallway at my mum's house. So emblematic of my dad. Just like his own dad whose trilby rode his coffin to the church on his last journey.

The holiday flats were my first real experience of the tourist trade and the amount of work that would go into making sure people's holidays were happy ones. Work that was done, not by some faceless automaton in the background, seamlessly and mechanically moving between mucky toilets and stained bedclothes, but by kids, families, people striving and stretching and grafting. My dad, and my mum, really cared about people having good holidays. People holidaying in Scarborough tended to be like us, not well-off. Holidays took months, sometimes years, of saving up for, and they knew that most of the people staying in their little block of holiday flats were people like them, who scrimped and saved for a week in Scarborough once or twice a year. One couple came for their honeymoon at the flats. My dad got up early on the morning after they arrived to bring them a platter with sausages and bacon and eggs, a gift to celebrate their new marriage. They didn't really know what to do with someone presenting them with a load of raw meat first thing in the morning, but it was the sort of traditional working-class thing that my dad really valued.

The flats were hard work for all of us. Every weekend my parents would wake us up – my older sister, my brother and me – and get us into whatever rust bucket we were driving at the time. We'd sit with the freshly ironed bedding across our knees, being poked in the back of the head with mop handles, the car filled with everything we'd need to clean four flats and welcome the guests. I was too little to be left at home on my own and I feel, looking back, that I was more of a nuisance than a help.

We'd work at manic speed, my mum checking the cleanliness of everything we did, getting us to clean again if it wasn't to the standard necessary for paying guests. The overriding memory is one of the deep, dark Victorian hallway, the smell of the sea washing through the house with all the windows open, the shush-shush of curtains blowing in the breeze, the constant sound of hoovering. And of the other blocks of holiday flats in the street doing the same – a row of open front doors like flags welcoming the holidaymakers, and after midday a clunk and thud and clank of cleaning equipment being loaded into parked cars as the owners prepared to go home. It all had to be done by midday when check-in began. After that we'd head upstairs to the attic, which had previously been done out as a bedsit. One of us would be in charge of making tea, one of us would be sent to the chippy round the corner with a list. Such anxiety to stand in the chip shop and tell them what I wanted, the embarrassment of asking for five fish to be fried, holding everyone else up. Then we waited. Mum or Dad would take us home, and one or the other of them would take the shift of waiting for guests to arrive.

Eventually, my dad got sick of the maintenance and eventually he sold the flats, just as property markets were on the rise. The flats sold for a profit and, combined with the money earned from the sale of our family home, my dad was finally able to buy his dream house and the small-holding – the chickens, the orchard and the koi pond he took such pride in.

Now my mum is struggling to look after the small-holding, and my dad's legacy is dissipating, and he is not here to witness it. I think about legacy a lot, especially in relation to my dad. He had hands that were permanently calloused from all the rough, manual graft he did, right from the age of fourteen, barely stopping. Even when he was so poorly, with a chemo line dangling out of his sleeve, he was still shifting piles of manure into the garden, digging and prepping vegetable beds, mowing lawns. It was in him, to be active, to be always in motion, to be always pushing back against something. It's so strange to have that furious energy gone, so suddenly, like the way that birdsong stops at the end of summer, how it is always slightly unexpected.

Later, I visit Scarborough, looking for the holiday flats. The sun is bright hot, and Scarborough is just as I remember it, blue skies, sunshine, the Edward Hopper shadows of the tall buildings. I identify the house. This street, and the ones that lead down to the seaside, were always lined with B&Bs and self-catering holiday flats. The traditional B&B has faded away and now there are far more Airbnbs in the area. I think 'our' old holiday flats might be apartments these days. I imagine the people in them no longer share a toilet and a bathroom. It probably costs quite a lot to live in an apartment this close to the sea, Peasholm Park and the town.

I have other memories of the area. Often, rather than get in the way of the cleaning regime, I would escape the dark hallways of the holiday flats to go and sit in Peasholm Park, feeding the squirrels and telling stories to myself. Peasholm Park was a magical place of fairy lights and swan boats and wildlife. I'd see water voles there, Canada geese, coots bobbing through the lily pads. It was a place of dappled light between huge trees, with secret gardens and fishponds hiding around secluded corners. The park was laid out in 1912, and was influenced by Japanese and Chinese styles, with a pagoda, sculptures and a lantern walk. The design of the park was based around Thomas Minton's 'willow pattern', a Chinoiserie pattern used on ceramic tableware. At the time it was seen as completely authentic, with Chinese workers hired as part of the construction team.

Part manmade and part nature, the park is unique in many ways. After the lake and the pedal boats, one finds oneself moving up through Peasholm Glen, following the route of Peasholm Beck. All around are giant trees. Each section has a tree-theme, different species specially collected and planted for the educated walker, at a time when science and nature were evolving together, and the world was being explored. The 'Forests of the World' walk includes 'Pine Forests of North America', 'Chinese Foothills', 'English Beech Wood', 'Slopes of Nepal' and 'Woodlands of New England'. There are over a thousand trees planted in the glen. They are wondrously tall in places, so much so that in the 1980s a bridge was built over the glen so that people could view the trees at eye level. In the 1990s, after a period of low funding, the now rundown and vandalized park received investment from the government, but it was a local community, 'the Peasholm Park Friends', who came to the rescue of this unique woodland. To be in the glen is to be away from the town. The sounds change to those of the forest, the senses dulled among the trees, the way that light and sound becomes muffled in a million piney branches. It feels secretive.

In 1994, a member of the Tree Register came to audit the trees of Peasholm Park. To his astonishment, he found several 'champion' trees. Champion trees are individual trees that are seen as exceptional examples of their species either due to their size, their rarity or their historical significance. In this case the champion trees were trees of significant girth and height, and the best examples of the species in the country. He also discovered two Dickson's Golden Elms, a tree thought to have become extinct during the Dutch Elm Disease outbreak in the 1970s. There is even a tree in the glen that defies identification, either by the Tree Register or indeed by Kew Gardens officials.

Truly, this place, planted for the amusement and delight of the people of Scarborough, is unique. The volunteers successfully bid for several small grants to help open up the woodland to the public and to make it accessible, creating a seating area and woodland walks so that people could identify the most special trees and connect to nature in a new and exciting way. I knew none of this as a child, roaming between these enormous trunks, looking for peace away from the grind of the Saturday cleaning schedule, and though I didn't know the history of the place, I still felt a connection to nature. I did not need to name the trees. I only had to reach out and touch the textured trunks, inhale the scent, or sit among them to connect to them, to find solace in the dappled light and the musky smell of bark.

The glen winds away and the park continues into the Victorian Dean Road and Manor Road cemeteries with their angels and anchor headstones. On this visit, I come here to remind myself of this place of solace, walking through the deep hush of the woods, past the tinkling beck and out into the cemetery, finding myself a ten-minute walk away from Woodlands Cemetery and my daughter. When you live in the same place all your life, everything becomes overlaid. Every time I peel back a layer of myself, here I am again, and here is my daughter, the catalyst for my reawakening.

At fourteen years old I got a doomed job waiting in a café on the seafront in Scarborough. Later, when I would find myself back working in shops and cafés as a nineteen-year-old, I would enjoy the experience of seasonal work. There were things I loved about working on the seafront. There was a proper buzz about it. It was a real way for me to enjoy a more social interaction too. There is something intimate about two co-workers at the end of the season, waiting for tourists to enter a café or a shop, waiting for orders to come into the kitchen. There is nothing to do but talk. In those spaces of quiet contemplation, my work friends and I would discuss our hopes for the future, our boyfriends, our families.

I worked a lot of different jobs in my teens and early twenties. In the first jobs, my co-workers were a mixed bunch of working-class and lower-middle-class people, from different schools around the town. These were people who I still think of fondly, but whom I will never see again, or if I do, they would be unrecognizable to me, like looking back at a diary excerpt and wondering what the context of the entries was. Some of these people were hoping for A-levels, university, careers.

One working-class girl I worked with, when I was first living with the Unsuitable Man, was much older than me at twenty or twenty-one. She was already living on her own, cherishing her independence. She wanted to be someone, wanted to go somewhere, was working so hard to get experience in the retail trade. She saw herself as management material and had a plan – she would push through anything to own her own house and car and be at the top of the chain. She'd made poor decisions early on after leaving school, but she was insanely driven, would turn up to work in smart business suits and ask to be put onto National Vocational Qualification (NVQ) training. I never saw her family – she never really talked about them, except to say that she wasn't really in touch with them anymore. Much, much later, when I worked in the laboratory, I came across her unusual name on a blood sample. It was a post-mortem sample. She had died of a heroin overdose, and I can remember being shocked, despite not having seen her for years, because she was the sort of girl who I assumed would ride her passion, her drive for life, to success. I never thought that this would be her end. I had been inspired by her, had gone on to do NVQs of my own in retail, holding the idea of her drive and passion for self-fulfilment in my head. What happened to her? I have no idea, but what I do know is that it is hard to break away from a life of feeling undervalued. To have a degree of self-validation is a brave thing for a girl whose family seemed to want nothing to do with her, a girl who decided to get out and work to strive. In this town, in seaside towns in general, people seem to roll towards the cliff edge seeking something beautiful, only to find the end of the earth and an expanse of deep blue nothing.

In the end, the waitressing job on Scarborough seafront was not for me. I lasted a miserable couple of days. I was far too shy for front of house. Any mistakes you made had to be paid for out of your own wages, so on the second day, when someone from West Yorkshire asked for a teacake, and I brought them what they called fruit bread, I lost a chunk of my wages. I was felled by dialect. Also I dropped a full tea tray and ruined the carpet in the back room. Also I asked some ladies if they wanted to see the Old Age Pensioner specials menu. Reader, they were not OAPs. Looking back, they were probably my age now. They were probably in their forties. They were aghast. No, waiting on was not for me.

The next job I got, when I was still fourteen years old, was in the kitchens at a hotel. I washed up, served food to the waitresses so they could take the dishes to the tables. Occasionally I changed bedding, moving from room to room along the vast corridors of the hotel. I cleaned toilets, again. I enjoyed the buzz of the kitchen environment, and when they suggested I try waiting on, I refused, much preferring the anonymity of the back kitchen, even if it was so hot it regularly made me feel faint, even if it was heavy work. (I once dropped an entire cottage pie made for twenty people because it was so hot and heavy my hand slipped in my own sweat.) But I will never forget picking up the brown envelope of my wage packet and finding actual folded notes inside, money that I had earned.

It was a real rite of passage and one of those times when I could feel genuine pride from my parents. I can't remember what I spent the money on. I did not save it like my parents wanted me to. I didn't buy clothes or music. I suspect I bought stationery and books. Unlike the school situation where people had their worth judged by their class, there was no real class divider when it came to after-school and weekend work. It's just what everyone did – everyone from a tourist town went to work and earned money. I have literally no idea if that is the same now, if anything has changed at all, but I suspect not. Perhaps it's the same everywhere. Come the summer season the tourist trade was insatiable, with jobs for everyone, a sudden, almost organic opening up of work, opportunity, but only for the season.

Once the seafront started shutting down – the arcade lights switched off, the wind blowing icy off the sea, the cafés, restaurants, hotels and bars slowing their pace – the work was gone. When winter comes to a seaside town, there is very little work. This is one of the things that keeps towns like Scarborough in a place of greater poverty. Lots of people want to move here to live in a gorgeous place – and who can blame them? – but they may have only ever been here in season while the town is bustling. People end up in Scarborough because nostalgia tells them they were happy here.

The reality of the town is that it is two towns, a picture card being flipped one way then another. The town out of season is a different beast altogether. It's why so many young people emerge from school ready to get out to university, if they're lucky, or inland to the cities, if they want to get anywhere or earn more than minimum wage. Everything is affected by this seasonal polarity. The council pours money into tourism, trying to keep the season alive for as long as it can, but the locals feel abandoned in the winter months. The town's population is skewed towards older people because so many retire here. But it means that the hospital struggles. Elderly folk come with the illnesses and pathology of the elderly, but if the seaside town hospital cannot retain staff, how can it cope? If there's no funding for amenities and pleasure activities for local people, out of season, who would stay? Not as many career-driven medical professionals will stay in a town that is closed half the year, when the alternative might be to live in Leeds or York, or one of the other vibrant cities in the north.

Property here is relatively cheap, compared to, for example, London. What would buy you a bedsit in London will buy you a six-bed detached house here. And many people with money can do just that, buy second homes. This, along with properties bought for Airbnb, pushes up property prices in general because affordable homes become less accessible, the demand outstrips the supply. In 2022 the average wage in Scarborough was around £28,000 per year, according to the Office of National Statistics.* The average house price in Scarborough is £220,465, according to *The Scarborough News* using data

---

* 'Earnings Gross Annual Time Series, Place of Work by Local Authority.' Office for National Statistics, 26 Oct. 2022.

from the Office of National Statistics.* But this is the *average*. Two people earning around £28,000 per year could possibly get a mortgage to buy that sort of house, but that's with the average wage. Working-class people primarily work in the tourist trade and will be earning far less than the average wage. They cannot afford to buy houses in the towns they come from, cannot afford to live in the towns they work in. This leads to fewer people working here and, out of season, the holiday homes create a ghost town, with buildings sitting empty.

Nearby, in the seaside town of Whitby, 28 per cent of the houses are holiday houses or second homes, according to a 2022 article in the *Guardian* newspaper.† In 2022, Whitby residents voted in favour to limit the number of second homes in the town. Although the ballot was not binding, it gives a good indication of the sense of power-lessness and upset that residents feel about the increase in second homes and holiday lets.

In some parts of Scarborough, the life expectancy of residents is much lower than the national average, and the levels of deprivation much higher, according to a 2023 Sky News report using data gathered by the Office for Health

---

* Buksmann, George. 'Check If House Prices Are Rising or Falling in Scarborough with This Interactive Tool.' *The Scarborough News*, 16 Feb. 2023, www.thescarboroughnews.co.uk/lifestyle/homes-and-gardens/are-house-prices-rising-or-falling-in-scarborough-check-the-local-property-market-with-our-interactive-tool-4029509.
† Halliday, Josh. 'Whitby Votes to Limit Sales of Second Homes.' the *Guardian*, Guardian News and Media, 14 June 2022, www.the guardian.com/uk-news/2022/jun/14/whitby-votes-to-limit-sales-of-second-homes.

Improvements and Disparities.* That Scarborough has one of the highest death rates from opioid abuse, that the town, for a while at least, was the drugs capital of the whole of the UK seems at odds with its pretty streets and beautiful views. People are buying up the fishing cottages and making many of them into highly desirable second homes, limiting the number of properties for sale and pushing the prices up far beyond what local people can afford. In some places gentrification has forced out the local community and, coupled with the poor management of the fishing industry, has meant there are fewer young people following their parents into the fishing trade. There are fewer opportunities to make a decent living and to be able to expand and grow a family-run business. There is less security in the fishing industry than there used to be. Many of the changes made in legislation are for the sake of conservation, which is surely a good thing, except that the people who experience those changes first-hand, the sons and daughters who cannot take on a family business because the rules are so much stricter and it is so much harder to make a profit, must adapt and change. I can't help but feel that it's so often the people at the bottom of the ladder who are forced to adapt and bear the brunt of change.

There is a pattern here. The poor get pushed out of their own lives, their own livelihoods. They are sent to the background, in their own landscapes, and the more

---

* Mahmood, Saywah, and Joely Santa Cruz. 'NHS at 75: The Parts of England with the Highest and Lowest Life Expectancies as Figures Reveal Health Postcode Lottery.' *Sky News*, 5 July 2023, news.sky.com/story/nhs-at-75-the-parts-of-england-with-the-highest-and-lowest-life-expectancies-as-figures-reveal-health-postcode-lottery-12913890.

privileged can observe that landscape as something quaint and desirable. In the past, these fishing towns, and the villages along the shores of Paleolake Flixton, were trading centres. The routes around the lake – the routes I've travelled on this day of bright sunshine where a few brave souls are beginning to wear shorts and sandals and the scent of sunscreen and ice cream waffles is just around the corner – were places of exchange. This trip into Scarborough has left me feeling nostalgic for my youth, but not for working in the tourist trade.

# CHAPTER NINE

# Waterways

For a long time, as I was growing up and growing into myself, I thought that the extinct lake, Paleolake Flixton, was actually an underground lake. I imagined that it existed in a great cavern like a Mexican cenote running deep and cool underground. I wondered how this huge lake just underneath the furrows and fields, the hedgerows and ditches of the valley, was safe to walk atop, how a tractor or a crop sprayer or a combine harvester could pass over without being lost to it.

I can picture myself as a child of nine or ten, in the back of the car, gazing out of the window as we drove along the western edge of the lake site, passing the hidden site of Star Carr on our way to wherever it was we were going. Perhaps we were on one of Dad's magical mystery tours up onto the Wolds, perhaps it was something more mundane than that.

As we passed the waterlogged fields that would have once been the edge of the lake, light slanted off the silvery puddles between tractor tyre tracks. My dad was saying

to my mum, *You know, there's an underground lake there.*
And I was soaking up the myth from the back seat.

It just so happened that as we were driving past the Star
Carr field, as my dad was saying this about the lake, I saw
a round concrete structure. It was raised, about five feet
tall, with a metal lid and a short metal ladder attached to
the side. It was wide enough for a person to open the lid
and enter it. I still don't know what these things are, and
I see them all the time around here. I suspect they are
drainage access points, or some sort of water source, but
when I saw the concrete roundel, my imagination took me
to an underground lake. A place stretching out beneath
the ground, dripping with stalactites, where the water was
an obsidian black and lapped at silent shores that no one
ever saw. The lake of my imagination was deep under the
earth and the only access to it was down that rusted ladder.
I never knew what my dad believed and what he didn't. I
have a feeling he may also have been told that the lake
existed as a tangible thing. But maybe it was all an act for
my sake.

When I think about my childhood, I think about my
dad, the proto-storyteller who, simply by the act of
recounting these strange and mysterious tales, encouraged
my imagination. At this point in my small life, the image
of the underground lake was set and the idea of that magical
place was difficult to shift. There was some disappointment
when I learned the true nature of the 'underground lake'
– it was simply a high-water table, a place where a body
of water may rise out of the earth and exist again. This,
then, is the real magic – the ghost lake rising, that to be
extinct is never to be fully extinct, that the land has archived
you, remembered you.

Later, researching for this book, I trawled through local

groups on social media networks. I wanted to know what local people thought about the lake. Occasionally the myth of the underground lake cropped up, especially when people had witnessed strange and seemingly inexplicable events in the area. One comment in particular struck me almost as a blueprint for how we humans make sense of terrible or inexplicable things by consigning them to myth.

Some years ago, a woman went missing in the area and was never seen again. I won't name her, because she is a real person, a person whose family and friends will still be suffering because of her disappearance. I don't know what the details were, only that she was last seen walking down a road I know well, in the early hours of the morning. I'm aware of her because her image appears on missing posters all over the local towns and villages. It is in the Chinese takeaway shop, in the entrance of one of the pubs in Filey, in the window of the bakery, in bus shelters, in the railway stations. This image, these posters, are regularly refreshed once the photo has faded in the sunshine, most likely by someone who loves her. Of course, social media is the place to spread information, lightning-quick. But social media is also a place of well-meaning misunderstandings and sometimes worse. One comment in one of the Facebook groups was written by someone wondering if she might have fallen into the underground lake. *Had she somehow fallen into a drainage ditch and disappeared?* The underground lake had allegedly taken tractors, had indeed almost taken two whole aeroplanes that crashed on the site during the Second World War. They were only just recovered before the boggy ground swallowed them. I read more comments online, and the gates creaked open wider and wilder theories came out. *Did you know there have been werewolf sightings? Did you know this area is a hot spot for UFO activity? Have you heard of the Wold Newton Triangle?*

This is how we explain the terrible and the unexplainable. But the wetlands in particular are a place of sustained ritual significance and have long attracted supernatural speculation. From the Mesolithic period onwards, people have focused on lakes and wetlands as a place for spiritual connection. Perhaps it is because the wetlands can be a life giver and a life taker. To safely navigate a wetland environment, one must know it intimately. To know where to place a foot, where to push a boat, where to catch a fish, where one might lose a life. A person lost in fenland may never be found. Perhaps this landscape memory lives on here.

The ghost lake transformed gradually over thousands of years, right up to the point of a manmade act of drainage in the nineteenth century. First there was the lake, a huge shimmer of water. Then, gradually, fenland, bog land, peat land – low and marshy, with deeper areas of water, places of deceptive grasses that could swallow a person. There are myths and stories of the fenland woven into our shared consciousness.

When the people of Germany and southern Scandinavia arrived here to settle, in the Early Medieval period, they were already used to the peaty fen environments and would have taken to this place well. Perhaps this is why there are so many Anglo-Saxon-sounding village names around the site. And the Anglo-Saxons came with their own fenland folktales.

In her book of tales from Early Medieval Britain, *Wild*, Amy Jeffs recounts the Old English poem of 'Wulf and Eadwacer'. In this story, two tribes live on islands in the fenland. They are locked in a long feud. Two characters

– an unnamed female narrator and a warrior from the opposing tribe, named Wulf – are in a secret relationship. Amy Jeffs is careful not to interpret the story as a love story – there is ambiguity in the roles of the female narrator and her could-be lover Wulf. What is clear is that the character of Wulf is the epitome of wildness, of freedom. He exerts a great pull over the narrator, who is unhappily married to a king in an opposing tribe. At one point, the protagonist sets out in search of Wulf in the fenland, gently taking a boat out among the reeds to meet him and plot their escape together. In the dead of night, in the blackness of the lake and the fens, she waits for Wulf. There is danger in the story – the narrator and Wulf must safely navigate the difficult terrain of the fenland, avoiding harm or death. Although the story is not set in northern England, I can imagine this lake, Paleolake Flixton, as the fenland setting. Perhaps the most famous Anglo-Saxon fen dweller is Grendel's mother, in *Beowulf*, who lives in a cave beneath a lake. There are so many monsters in the in-between places, the liminal spaces of fenlands, marshes and bogs, places of uncertainty and the unknown.

The lake area has a long and complex history, long enough for legends to be created and for myths to become embedded in the community. As early as the tenth century, wolves were recorded as a problematic presence in the area. Across the Wolds and the valley, wolves and wolf attacks were so ubiquitous that a hospital was built to protect travellers from being killed by the animals, who were particularly keen on eating those who passed along the trade routes between towns. Perhaps this is where the legend of the Flixton werewolf comes from, handed down through the centuries.

The beast, called Old Stinker, is rumoured to be at least

six foot tall, with glowing red eyes and breath that smells of rotting flesh, hence the name. If you do a quick internet search of 'Old Stinker', you'll see that Hull, a city on the coast in East Yorkshire, about an hour's drive away from the lake site, had a resurgence of werewolf sightings in 2016. One vivid account involves the beast allegedly eating a German Shepherd. This werewolf was also called Old Stinker, and the theory goes that the Flixton werewolf and the Hull werewolf are one and the same, Old Stinker expanding its territory to satiate its hunger. The last alleged sighting of Old Stinker in Flixton was in 2015 at Staxton roundabout, on the crossroads just outside the village.

Perhaps the werewolf is a reflection of our widespread anxiety. If we look at what was happening in 2015, around the time of the last sighting, we see that the UK was building up to the Brexit referendum. The country was fizzing with tension and unease. The voting results in Yorkshire and Humberside were 1,158,298 to remain and 1,580,937 to leave. In this area in particular, farmers, fishermen and rundown hospitals were being promised a miracle cure from Brexit, and they voted predominantly leave.

My point is, when Old Stinker re-emerged, it was during a time of fear and uncertainty. It is as if the myth was wrenched from the common consciousness to take the place of a fear that was difficult to conceptualize. People were angry, they wanted change, but I'm struck by how often that change was something people – politicians, voters, people on the street – found difficult to articulate. And when we find it difficult to articulate our fears, we create myths and legends to take the place of that abstract fear. We transfer the fear to something that can be vilified or hunted or protected against, rather than something unknowable, unseeable. I feel there is something else going on with the werewolf myth too. The landscape holds its legends and its myths, and this landscape is one where the past collides with the present. These places have remained the same for thousands of years, and folktales and myths have been passed along through generations.

I'm thinking again about the people of Star Carr and the ritual deposits of deer skull headdresses. Ethnographic research shows other cultures using similar deer skull head-dresses in ceremonies in which the person in the headdress 'becomes' the animal. There is a re-enactment of the animal's behaviour. The wearer is perhaps a shaman, who performs a ritual dance, mimicking the sound of hooves, tossing their head, stamping their foot until the people watching in the flickering firelight can see a merging of animal and human, a new creation, a hybrid between man and nature. Tapping into the animal psyche, the hunter becoming the hunted, the hunted becoming the hunter. And then the act of deposition, a physical link to the magic of that transformation left in the water, to the gods of the underworld. Research collated by Professor Nicky Milner's team suggests that during the early Holocene, the period in which Star Carr was inhabited, a period in which the climate was unstable, ritual deposits increased. This might indicate a kind of ritual offering or appeasement.

I'm speculating, but this is nothing new. People have been speculating about the history of the lake for centuries. At one time, flint tools that emerged out of the ground were thought to be from the fairies or hobgoblins. They were thought to make cattle lame, to cast some sort of spell or curse. At one time tumuli were thought to be the homes of dragons guarding treasure.

There are other bodies of water that attracted prehistoric

communities. The Gypsey Race was important to the prehistoric people living in the area. They built their burial mounds on its curves. The stream was probably special to them because of its sporadic rising. Winterbourne streams and rivers are dry in the summer months and usually rise in the winter months, at times when there has been no excessive precipitation. They are formed in areas with porous rocks, like chalk. The Gypsey Race was once known as the 'woe water', rising only, it was said, at times of national pain. It rose during the great plague of 1665 and in both the First World War and the Second World War. The last time it rose was in 2012, when it rose so high it flooded the village of Burton Fleming.

When I lived in Bridlington with the Unsuitable Man, we lived in an attic flat above the point where the woe waters ran out into the sea. It was not a good relationship. I had not yet learned to know my own worth. I let my heart be broken, and break it he did, with some relish, it seemed to me at the time. I felt myself drawn to the woe waters then, and the myth of their rising, wondering whether the constant flow of woe over the weir beneath our flat had caused our unhappiness.

I was a shy, vulnerable twenty-year-old dating an entirely unsuitable twenty-seven-year-old man. I'd met him and moved in with him when I was seventeen. A chunk of my precious teenage years was lost to the relationship. Eventually, I found a tiny chink of self-reliance. I got a job in a cake factory and made friends. When I broke up with the Unsuitable Man, my own woe waters rose in me. I was left on my own in our flat. He'd taken the furniture when he left, so I had nothing but a mattress, a tiny TV and my imagination. I imagined myself doing interesting things, things that didn't rely on the will of another person, a man. As I lay on the bare mattress in the tiny attic we'd once shared, I dared to imagine a different kind of life, one where I might be something else, someone else. I started writing. Perhaps the woe of the woe waters was necessary. A friend, rather than a foe. In the end, I was washed back out across the Wolds to the valley, to my parents' house on the edge of the lake.

The myths that circulate in this part of Yorkshire go further still. Or rather the myths have been teased out to create a web, a triangle of mysteries tenuously linked by the landscape. That web of mysteries is known as the Wold Newton Triangle, and the ghost lake itself sits right in the middle of it. The Gypsey Race flows through the triangle, which is pitted with howes and tumuli, the burial mounds of the prehistoric people who lived here. In Rudston, a ten-minute drive from the lake, the tallest standing stone in England sits in the middle of a churchyard, not far from the Gypsey Race. This Neolithic monument was known in the past as 'the devil's needle'. It's another example of local mythmaking. Now known as the Rudston Monolith, it is perhaps one of the most impressive places within the Wold Newton Triangle. The territory of the Wold Newton Triangle contains the myths of Old Stinker, the Spital Hospital, the Gristhorpe man (a Bronze Age chieftain found in an oak coffin on the cliffs above the village of Gristhorpe), the dragon at Filey Bay (whose teeth were sealed shut by Yorkshire parkin) and the Wold Newton meteorite. The meteorite fell in 1795, landing a few feet from a ploughman. It embedded itself in the chalk ground in a metre-wide crater. The triangle of the Wold Newton Triangle is arbitrary; it's only a triangle if you want it to be one. A person could look at any area in Britain and find a selection of misunderstood events – mounds, beacons, standing stones

– and place them into a triangle; a shape that seems to lend itself to mythmaking. But the myths themselves shouldn't be simply brushed aside. After all, myths and folklore hold kernels of truth. Before we knew about ancient man, about civilizations that had been here before us, how would we know what a tumulus was, or why an arrowhead made of flint might emerge from the ground, or how a wolf, just an ordinary wolf, might be so clever and so quick as to trap a traveller and kill him? Perhaps, for people in the valley, and over the Wolds where between the villages was a great black night, the myths were a way of defining something unknowable, and gaining a sense of control as a result.

I was the monster in my own myth, always skirting on the edges, never quite belonging. What stories did I tell myself about my place in the world? What myths did I internalize? What woe waters did I carry inside of me? The biggest myth that I told myself was that I was broken, that to lose a baby, to be infertile, was to be something monstrous. When I was with child, I felt connected to the world in a way I'd longed for. I felt I finally belonged, wild and natural and completely balanced as if everything that was bad about me was offset by something incredibly precious, a rare goodness. When I lost my daughter, it was confirmation of my long-held belief that I did not belong, that there was something off and odd about me, something monstrous and black inside that would not allow my daughter to thrive. Something that prevented me from securing a PhD or having a family of my own or being truly loved.

My daughter gave me a gift. I couldn't see it then – it's taken years of digging into myself, of being an archaeologist in my own internal landscape to really see it. She gave me the gift of myself, my authentic self. That great wild grief was the first time I'd seen the myths that I had created around who I was, and I was able to peel them away. Through that destructive grief, I had seen a glimpse of my true self.

I'm sitting at my desk. It is one of those late spring evenings when summer is almost within touching distance. The swifts are flickering past the windows, the blackbird is singing at the edge of the garden. On my wall, a quote from *Bring Up the Bodies* by Hilary Mantel. *The things you think are the disasters in your life are not disasters really. Almost anything can be turned around: out of every ditch, a path, if you can only see it.*

## CHAPTER TEN

# Wolf Land

I'm sitting in my car in the car park of the Spital Farm Camping Site and Themed Shopping Centre. It's early June and I have the door open, enjoying the warmth of the sunshine. There's still a chill in the air if you're standing in shadow, but I can feel the summer arriving shyly. On the way here I had the window down, listening to the screech of swifts as they swooped and fluttered over the ghost lake, picking off the insects above the fields. The first hay cuts have already happened across the carrlands. Thick, lush grass for silage is lying in satisfying ridges, waiting to be bagged up for storage. The great fields of oilseed rape that blanket the landscape, so shockingly yellow just a week ago, are beginning to wane, the colour bleeding away, the seed pods beginning to bulge. The air is still thick with the scent of hawthorn blossom, but the petals are starting to break away now, constellations on tarmac and car roofs and sticking to the brown heads of bullrushes.

I'm uncharacteristically early for an appointment with

my hairdresser, and I've stopped to watch a rookery in the tops of the trees that line the road to Seamer. The sound of crows feels primal – there's something ancient to the grating, echoing call. Rookeries can remain in the same area for hundreds of years. Mark Cocker, in his book *Crow Country*, describes one colony in Dumfriesshire that could be traced back to the 1650s. They are often to be found on estate land, land belonging to or surrounding country houses, the quiet places where the public are not permitted. Few can come and disturb them. Sometimes the colonies are left over as the world changes around them, leaving pockets of crows surrounded by roads and buildings. There's one like this near my own village, in the grounds of a seventeenth-century hall. The colony hangs over a busy road – the fledglings are often to be found fallen out of the trees, smashed to pieces by cars or standing forlornly in the gutter. Why do they keep coming back? Why do they keep nesting in such a precarious place? I imagine the rookery has been there for hundreds of years, but the road has got busier and busier beneath them.

The rookery I'm watching now is in a line of trees, five or six trees deep, that stretches along the side of a busy road, one of the main roads into Scarborough. The road runs along the west side of the lake site, passing the Mesolithic settlement of Star Carr. It is right next to a major crossroads, with a roundabout that sends people north, east and west. I'm wondering, as I sit here, what this rookery might have seen, what changes have happened beneath it as the crows squabbled and clattered through the trees.

Today's pilgrimage takes me to Flixton again, and a long-gone medieval hospital that was built to be a place of safety for travellers fleeing wolves on the Wolds. It just so happens that Spital Farm Camping Site and Themed

Shopping Centre is also built on the site of a hospital, a coincidence, but also another indicator of the rich history of this area. The medieval 'hospital' was not a hospital as we might know it – a place to treat sick people – but rather a place for 'hospitality' in its truest sense; a place for travellers to take shelter at night if they were between towns and villages.

Thomas Hinderwell, a notable historian, most famous for descriptions of Scarborough and the surrounding area, mistook Spital Farm for the Folkton hospital. He states in his 1811 book *The History and Antiquities of Scarborough, and the Vicinity*:

> At Flixton, a village farther inland [than Hunmanby] at the foot of the Wolds, an hospital was founded in the reign of Athelstan, of which the following account is given in Dugdale's *Monasticon*:
>
> 'The charter of the 25th VI. shows that one Achorne, Lord of Flixton in the parish of Folkton, in the reign of King Athelstan, built this hospital for one alderman and fourteen brothers and sisters at Flixton aforesaid, for the preservation of people travelling that way, that they might not be devoured by wolves and other wild beasts then abounding there; endowing the said hospital with several possessions at Flixton, which were afterwards augmented by other benefactions, and confirmed by the aforesaid King Henry, who also enjoyed that, according to ancient custom, the vicar of Folkton should say solemn mass in the Hospital-chapel on the feast of St. Andrew, and after such mass should bless bread and water, and divide and sprinkle it among the people then present, to whom several indulgences were granted by the popes.'

There is a certain parcel of land in this vicinity distinguished by the name of Wolf-Land; and on the spot where the Hospital anciently stood, is now a Farm-house called Spital.

I think about this as I make my way to have my hair coloured. I can't help but feel a thrill when I enter the building, knowing the history of the site. This is the type of historical connection I like, to be able to see a continuity of landscape, and the way people engage with a place. As I get out of the car I can see the earthworks that indicate field systems and foundations of a building that would have been run like a monastery.

My hairdresser's salon is, I think, in the modern part of the building, though the old fold yard of the farm is merged into a great modern barn, within which a whole town of mock Victorian cobbled streets, bow-fronted shops and cafés has been created. It makes it difficult to tell what is authentic and what is not. The back of the salon is chalk brick, as far as I can see, so that might be a leftover from the older buildings.

Corrine, my hairdresser, is one of those people who seems completely at ease with others. She is a people person, knowing when to ask questions, when to not, when to support, when to step away. She moves around me, carefully colouring and cutting. We move into the back of the salon, and she carefully places me in the chair there, and I lean into the pillowed edge of the round basin. She continues chatting about her boys, about her work, about mutual friends and acquaintances and then, when she washes my hair, she quiets, massaging my scalp as she works the conditioner in. I feel my muscles untense, my neck makes a series of internal crackles and snaps as it relaxes. To have someone take the time to make you look and feel good about your-self, someone who recognizes that to be close to a person, to find out how you can make them feel better about themselves, is a form of healing and that to heal and help in a way that isn't necessarily medical is important. Visits to the hairdresser give me permission to stop and let someone else take responsibility for me, even if it's just for a couple of hours. It is like stepping out of my life of books and documents, workshops and feedback, worry and internal questioning, and allowing myself to be cared for.

I am not a people person. I have terrible social anxiety and struggle to understand what is expected of me in social situations, and it took some time for me to find a hairdresser who just worked with that, who added something to my life, something I perhaps didn't know that I needed. Corrine does this, carrying out this small act of care for her clients in this small salon in this building where women – given most physical, medical and emotional care has always been done by women – spent hundreds of years bathing, caring for and healing those in need.

I leave the hairdresser's with my hair pinker. I'm growing into my now natural silver and white hair, adding a lot of pink for dramatic effect. This is a halfway step for me, a step towards acceptance. This is the longest I have kept the same colour scheme and style since I was a child with hair that refused to be tamed. I have always had a habit of having radical hairstyles in times of stress, especially when facing big events or challenges I didn't feel strong enough to cope with, especially when entering the largely middle-class arena of the arts. I think it is a way of creating a different personality, a kind of mask that would allow me to face the world as a slightly different person. A person, for example, with a shaved head and big blocky glasses cannot possibly be too shy to speak at a script-in-hand reading of their own play, can they? I suspect the decision, or rather the desire, to stay with the same hair colour and cut says something about my journey towards accepting myself, being someone who doesn't need that sort of armour anymore. That said, I did just have a conversation with Corrine about cutting back on the silver and running pink underneath for when the book comes out and I need to do promotion. Maybe I have not travelled that far away from the girl who feels she never fits in. Either way, I feel 100 per cent better about my appearance now than when I went into the hairdresser's. I am rested in a way that I find hard to categorize. This is the power of a good hairdresser.

I drive back to Flixton, a three-minute drive, and park up on North Street again, facing into the lake site. I feel like this place, in the centre of the lake, has become central to my personal journey. I have learned of the horse bones of my land ancestors, the places where farming was uprooted, where labourers were left without work, where the pandemic is remembered and now the site of the Flixton hospital, where people fled from wolves.

I walk down to the end of the road, crossing the tamed Hertford. I want to unpick time and imagine this road the way the travellers would have seen it in the tenth century when the hospital was founded. I can see the small chalk paths that lead down from the Wolds, hollowed with time, and the fields, earthworks, chalk pits, and the steep rise of the valley. The hospital was called Carman's Spital. 'Carman' is an old word for someone who delivers goods via horse-drawn cart, or on horseback. This hospital, I'm sure, would have cared for the sick and the needy, but its main purpose, its reason for being created, was to protect travellers. There is a passage translated from a tenth-century charter in *An Historical and Descriptive Guide to Filey* by William Smithson, published in 1861, that mentions the hospital:

> . . . by the authority and permission [of] the said king, establish a hospital for one alderman and fourteen brethren and sisters, within the said Flixton, for the preservation of persons travelling in the neighbour-hood, lest they should be devoured by wolves and other voracious wild beasts then existing there . . .

The king referred to is Athelstan, who reigned between 924 to 939. It's a complicated reign because, for part of it, he ruled in just one area of the country, and for the latter part he was acknowledged as the King of the English. The charter goes further, mentioning the conditions in winter, when the lake, the carr and the small bodies of lake water known as 'meres' would have flooded, making the area dark and dangerous to anyone who did not know it intimately. William Smithson's translation of the original charter states:

> . . . and now various of the lieges travelling near the hospital by night or in winter, would perish in waters, swamps and marshes, if they had not the hospital there.

What is important to me is the mention of the meres. In winter, this part of the UK is dark by 4 p.m., the sun not fully risen before 9 a.m. When the weather is bad, it feels darker. I have seen the lake site at night when the village lights ring its edges. I almost can't imagine what this place would be like without those lights, how terrifying it would be to cross through the surrounding forests, where the wolves were so many and so clever that they spawned a legend in the form of a werewolf, and then to cross the marshy landscape, with its series of black, freezing pools, trying to get to safety.

William Smithson, in his 1861 guide to Filey, claims that the very name of Flixton village is derived from the fact that it was a place to flee. As I understand it: *Flucht-ton*. From Old High German and proto-German, the tongue of the Saxons so well known here, '*Fluhti*' meaning 'to escape', '*Fliehen*' meaning 'to flee'. Perhaps the low, thatched houses and the long halls of the village, clustered around North Street and the Malton Road, were already places to run to, out of those thick woods, into a village where wolves might not come, a place with guard dogs and houses with thick chalk walls, a place with a fire burning brightly in a hearth. Perhaps the villagers complained that they were always having to take in terrified travellers fleeing wolves. It would make sense then for the lord of the manor, a knight named Acehorn, to petition for a place of refuge to be built.

There is an old story, often attributed to Native Americans, but according to that great knowledge source Wikipedia more likely to be Christian in origin. In the tale, a grandfather advises his grandson on how to deal with good and evil. To paraphrase:

The grandfather tells his grandson, 'There are two wolves battling inside us. One seeks only peace and light and asks to be at one with the world around it, at peace in nature and going about its life calmly, happily. The other is full of anger and hatred towards others or towards things that cannot be changed. This wolf's whole world is focused on the anger it feels, and it sees nothing of the world except for how the world has hurt it.'

'Which wolf will win the battle?' asks the little boy.

The grandfather replies, 'The one you feed.'

I can relate to this fable. I have been fleeing the angry wolf inside me for so many years, and for many years I fed her. My daughter died, in part, from clinical negligence, and the wolf that experienced the preventable loss of my child was an angry one. Some days it felt like I could open my mouth and howl. Sometimes I did, while out walking in the lanes, alone, when everyone else was at work. I would cry in anger and frustration and terrible grief.

I was a wolf mother too, protecting my daughter in death. It was much easier to inhabit this wolf form. The wolf felt justified in her anger. She came to meetings about my daughter's autopsy with bared teeth. This wolf growled and ambushed and attacked. This wolf needs thanking. She protected me, and she got me through the hardest times of my life. But now I am conscious that the hard graft of the early years of grief is past, that I need to be accountable for my own sense of peace.

When I first began to think about life as a childless woman, I tried to flee the angry wolf. I tried to ignore her, while she wound around me, making me bitter with the things I felt I couldn't say for fear of upsetting or offending people. Eventually I found that a wolf that lives within you cannot be ignored. I have been hurt, and it is not simply about *looking at the positives* or *not dwelling*, it is about acknowledging the angry wolf, but feeding the other wolf. Or, perhaps, stretching the analogy a little too far – feeding both wolves and accepting both wolves are part of my pack. The other wolf is vulnerable. She creeps around the edges of society. Sometimes she is shooed away, sometimes she is not welcome. But she too is capable of survival. It is survival in an entirely different manner. She is the wolf I am reaching for now. I am neither the traveller fleeing, nor the wolf attacking, but the wolf in the hills. The wolf in the wild making her own way through the world.

Carman's Spital had one alderman, an overseer of the running of the hospital, and fourteen brethren and sisters, monks and nuns there to provide care and run the hospital. It had a chapel, and would have been monastic in style, probably a brick building, probably built from the local chalk in the local style. Perhaps one of the farms here sits on its foundations, perhaps the buildings have repurposed the original stones. The hospital was awarded land by the king at the time for them to grow crops, fuel for fires and to raise animals to eat. William Smithson's translation continues:

> . . . and did endow the said alderman, brethren, and sisters, with a certain toft, one croft, and two selions of moor and pasture, with their pertinents, in Flixton aforesaid; and granted them common pasturage sufficient for twenty-four cows and one bull, in certain place there called 'Forthside' as far as 'Lingholm', round a certain place called Staxton Mere as far as the boundary of Muston . . .

The places that are named in this extract are near to where my own village is. These are the places that I walk my old dog on a daily basis, and it pleases me to find this connection, and a new lens to view this familiar area through. I imagine myself walking between the layers of history, my old dog at my side. It's interesting to see the meres mentioned – Staxton Mere, Muston Mere – as it indicates that at this time the lake was still, in places, a big enough body of water to be named as such, rather than fenland or bogland. I can imagine coracles, small round boats made by fenland people, being used to fish and cross these bodies of water, and the eels and fishes and waterfowl that would have been native here. I like to make that connection, to imagine a link between the medieval village inhabitants and the Mesolithic people who also used small boats to get to the islands in the lake. If I walk out of my village and down to the River Hertford, I can look almost in a line right up to Folkton and Flixton. Now I shall stand on the bridge and imagine the villages, the meres and Carman's Spital, the ringing of a bell to call the hour, the sound of wolves howling in the woods.

It is thought that wolves arrived in the United Kingdom around twelve thousand years ago from mainland Europe. At Star Carr, during the 2015 excavations, two full wolf skulls were found among the deposits in the lake. The wolves in Britain were Eurasian wolves, a wolf breed that differs from its American timber wolf cousins by a straighter face, a coat that has more reds and browns in it and a softer, haunting call. A Eurasian wolf can be 180 pounds and six feet tall on its hind legs. The common misconception is that wolves are like dogs. But wolves are like wolves – they are wild, intelligent and enormous, and we have forgotten our place with them, forgotten to respect them.

In winter, wolf attacks were particularly bad. The *Anglo-Saxon Chronicle* states that January was known as 'wolf-monat' by the Anglo-Saxons because, in mid-winter, with little other sustenance to be had, wolves devoured people. It was the most dangerous month for travellers.

Wolves are opportunistic and, like all animals, have a strong survival instinct. Accounts of wolves digging up recently buried corpses in graveyards at times of extreme hunger are widespread. In Scotland in 1846, the problem was so bad that the inhabitants of Eddrachillis, a parish in the county of Sutherland, resorted to burying their dead on islands. In *A Book of Highland Minstrelsy* from 1846, there is a poem devoted to the dangers of the wolf and the horrors of its habits:

Thus every grave we dug
The hungry wolf uptore,
And every morn the sod
Was strewn with bones and gore;

No wonder they spawned nightmarish legends and myths.

It was Athelstan, who sanctioned Carman's Spital, who also imposed annual wolfskin tributes. Wolves' deaths became a means of currency, a way of paying dues, doing one's part for society. Hunmanby, the village within walking distance from Flixton, is named after the wolf hunters there: Hunts-man-by. The Wolds were famous for the number of wolves that lived there, and for wolf hunters. Hunters were given land as a reward if they killed enough wolves, and slowly but surely wolves were eradicated from Britain.

By the reign of Henry VII in the late fifteenth century, wolves were becoming rare, but so prolific was the wolf in East Yorkshire over the Wolds, that, according to Joseph Strutt, author of *The Sports and Pastimes of the People of England*, wolf bounties were still being maintained until well into the nineteenth century. As the landscape evolved from forest and carr to farmland, there were fewer places for wolves to live, fewer places to hunt, fewer places to hide. It seems that this steady loss of habitat was the death knell for wolves in East Yorkshire.

Now the forest is all but gone, with managed woodland and forestry in isolated pockets between fields of livestock and crops. The once wild landscape is carefully controlled. We are no longer at the mercy of other animals. We have conquered the landscape, and in doing so have eradicated much of the wildlife.

When I was a child, whenever we would travel anywhere in the car, the windscreen was always pasted with dead insects. This is an anecdotal baseline, and a gross one. Now, as a person living and working in the exact same environment, travelling to the same places as I did in my youth, I rarely have to clean my windscreen on my return. There are very few flies smeared across the window. Anecdotal it may be, but this is real and lived experience of our declining insect population. It is known as the 'windscreen phenomenon', and in 2022 the Bugs Matter Citizen Science Survey was released by a group of organizations including the Kent Wildlife Trust. This study measured the number of dead bugs on vehicle number plates and recorded this information to assess the population of bugs in areas across the UK. The number of insects sampled from vehicles in 2019 and 2021 was compared to a nationwide survey using the same method conducted by the Royal Society for the Protection of Birds (RSPB) in 2004*. The comparison revealed a decrease in the number of insect splats on vehicles in the UK of 63.7 per cent.

---

* Ball, Lawrence. 'The Bugs Matter Citizen Science Survey.' *Bug Life*, Kent Wildlife Trust, 2022, kentwildlifetrust.org.uk/bugs-matter.

There are lots of factors that must be considered with such a survey. As a scientist, a biologist, I can see that this method of data collection is not ideal. It doesn't account for wind speed and car speed, for example, but it does tie in with what people working and living in rural areas have been saying: there are fewer insects. There are fewer birds. Wildlife populations are declining. What does this have to do with wolves and their eradication? Arguably, quite a lot.

Insects are near the bottom of the food chain, but they serve a crucial role. They are the foundations on which our lives depend and with the changing of the environment, the industrialization of farming methods, the control and subjugation of the wild environment to a maintained and managed landscape that benefits humans only, we are slowly killing ourselves. The changing landscape that eradicated the wolf, along with other dangerous 'beasts', is limiting the biodiversity, and we will suffer for it, along with all other animals and plants. We already are suffering. We are frogs boiling in a pan, not noticing as the water heats around us. We are hardwired to normalize new situations, new environments, new stresses. What has caused the reported 63.7 per cent decline in insects stated in the Bugs Matter study? In rural areas it is most likely due to intensive farming methods and habitat loss. The Bugs Matter report states:

> . . . insect abundance may be low in these locations due to pesticide use, the negative influence of crop monocultures on insect abundance, a lack of habitat attributes that provide nesting or overwintering habitats, and a lack of undisturbed habitat and habitat continuity due to intensive management for crops . . .

There are more studies, more data collections, more correlations and explorations about what is happening in our environment and yet each year very little is done about it. Between climate change and industrialization of the environment, we are burning the fuse to our own demise.

I think about the time my dad, as a child, watched the farm owner tear down the orchard at the back of their tenant farm to provide more square footage of farmland. I remember that, at seventy, it still upset him. The trees, their fruit potential, the places where the birds nested, all gone, burned down using old engine oil, billowing black smoke into the air.

Sometimes, when I can see the evidence of our declining world, I am thankful that I likely won't witness its end. I'm grateful to have experienced the world nearer the beginning of that decline. I'll be dead before the birdsong disappears, because it is coming, and God help my niece and nephews, and the generations that follow us.

# CHAPTER ELEVEN

# The Road Home

I moved away from home when I had just turned seventeen. I had left school, avoided being funnelled into factory work or shop work, and decided against sixth form, or progression of education. I imagine, from the outside, I must have seemed awkward, difficult to motivate. From the inside, I was desperately relieved to be away from school and the constant un-fitting-in-ness of it all. The relief of having time, at least for a week or so, to lie on my bed and read books was like being plunged into a pool of cool, still water after being rolled and smashed about in the waves.

There was a short period of time, after I'd left school, in which nothing was really expected of me, I did not have to confront anything, didn't have to battle the anxiety, didn't have to fix myself or change myself to fit in. I stayed in the tiny boxroom which I had chosen when my brother moved out, because of the morning light that fell into it from over the fields of wheat on the other side of the street. We had house martins nesting under the eaves, and this bedroom window was the one they nested next to. I would carefully open the window and lay my head on the sill, staying perfectly still to watch them flit in and out, the curious, domed heads of the chicks appearing above the cement of spit and mud.

That summer I walked the fields. I walked the dog. My mind was empty of everything. I didn't know who I was or what I wanted. I read *Wuthering Heights*, I read *Jane Eyre*, I wrote in my diary the thoughts of a self-conscious sixteen-year-old who felt self-conscious even writing to herself. Even in my own diary, I pretended to be the sort of person who wrote in a diary, someone normal whose thoughts weren't strange or weird.

One day, my mum harried me from my room and talked to me about getting a job, afraid, I imagine, that I would fall down the cracks and end up without work. *It's easier to use your brain than your hands.* I think of her, the girl that she once was, younger than me when she went to night school to learn how to type, how to keep books, how to write shorthand, how it meant that she used her brain and not her hands and avoided the physical strain of manual labour. How she was shepherding me towards something similar.

I began applying for junior office roles. I am surprisingly good in interviews. I found that if I just pretended to be the kind of person who would be ideal for the job, then I usually got that job. I had taken my GCSEs in a haze of utter anxiety and had done far worse than expected. My coursework saved me. But still, I had basic GCSEs, I could file, I could do office work. I was bright. I could take instruction. I got jobs and was excited, initially, about the person I might be. A person who would wear the beautiful business suits and heels and use folders and clipboards and sit at their own desk, in their own space, typing and chatting and going out for drinks with the girls. That person was the person who had done the job interview. It wasn't me. What I found was that I spent the whole time in a prison of shyness, unable to talk to people, unable to use the phone confidently, avoiding it when I could, staring out at the plants in the car park, longing for the outside.

The office culture was toxic to me. I felt bullied, I couldn't fit in, and once again I did not belong. Again, here were the crushing, sickening mornings of getting dressed, pushing myself forward to this place where somehow something made me vulnerable to pranks and jokes and gossip and shouting. It was exhausting. And then along came the Unsuitable Man, who caught me like a fish at a fairground, hooking me out and carrying me away. I left home, left my job and went with him, allowed myself to be led away.

I pretended then to be the girlfriend, the happy, in-love girl, and he tried to be the good boyfriend, until he didn't. I drifted along with him, like a deflated balloon, and the relationship worsened. We moved into town, and we kept moving between flats. I lived, for a while, with heroin addicts. I lived, for a while, with drug dealers. We moved to Bridlington. I didn't become a ghost of myself because I didn't know who I was. I just became a fainter version of the ghost I was. The drug-taking increased and the drinking increased and, if I was in a movie, I would say, *This is the part of my life I call misery* because it was.

He couldn't keep a job, my jobs didn't pay enough. Eventually I applied for work in a cake factory and went to the interview as someone who might work in a cake factory and got the job and found, to my absolute delight, that I loved it. It was well paid, the people I worked with were welcoming, interesting and from all walks of life.

They were students funding their studies, professional chefs now too old for the hard labour of restaurant kitchen life, ex-cons and cake-lifers, women and men to whom the factory was a second home. There was a sense of community, and I found myself with work friends. The work itself was monotonous, the noise of the machines so loud everyone was given ear protectors. You couldn't talk during work time because you couldn't hear each other. We stood at our stations on the gateaux line and frisbeed cake disks onto the moving conveyor. We moved position every thirty minutes and after one full circuit it was breaktime, coffee in the canteen, then the system started again. I loved the simplicity of it. I could tell myself stories and simply exist, and I didn't need to do anything except be a cog in a machine. We got paid well. We got good holidays. We got up at four in the morning, but I was an early riser anyway, leaving the Unsuitable Man in bed, surrounded by Special Brew cans.

I would get dressed, washed, creep out into the just-rising sun and walk along the promenade where the sea rolled along the shore, and the world was my own, completely my own, until I boarded a bus, and the other workers were there. One colleague in particular caught me up. He was reading Shakespeare on the bus. I managed to rake up a couple of lines from my GCSE *Henry V* and quoted them. This then became a game. He would quote a line, I would quote one back. When he worked on the same assembly line as me, I'd lift my head and see him watching. This was what the first inklings of love might have been. Except he had a girlfriend that I didn't know about. And then one day we came to work and found out he'd died by suicide. Some black despair was in him that we couldn't see.

That's when things began to come apart, or rather, that was a catalyst for things speeding up – the drink, the drugs, the terrible relationship – until one day I stood at the window in the tiny attic flat and asked the Unsuitable Man to leave. He threatened suicide if we broke up and when I didn't react, didn't leap to save him, he didn't end his life. He left. He took the furniture, and I didn't stop him. I had burned myself down to a stub with it all. I kept the portable TV, a mattress and a tiny 1.5-seater sofa. I walked to the phone box at the end of the road, because we didn't have a phone, and called in sick from the factory for two weeks with terrible flu, and I lay on my mattress in the tiny room and cried and wanted to die from the sadness.

Eventually, I phoned my sister, and she came, and we had a day out. She bolstered my confidence. When I returned to work at the factory with its constant heartbeat of conveyor belts and the warm smell of cakes, my colleagues' well-meaning advice was to try again with the Unsuitable Man. In a moment of revelation, I realized that if I did, if I went back to being an object in his life, I would never move on, I would never move up and perhaps, just perhaps, I wasn't meant to be this unhappy.

The Unsuitable Man was running away from himself. I think about him now, what he might be doing, wherever he is, and I hope he found the thing that would give him worth. I hope he found it inside himself, found that he could be worthy of his own love. But I was not a rehabilitation centre for him. I decided to come home, though I wasn't sure what home meant. I knew that I wanted to be back in the comfort of a familiar landscape. I quit my job and returned to my parents' house. As we drove the coast road home, and through Hunmanby, the village of the wolf hunters, and down into the valley, my heart sang to see the lake site again, the villages and Seamer Beacon on the horizon; whale-backed and bristled with trees.

I met my husband-to-be a year or so later. He tamed me as if he was taming a deer; carefully, gently, holding out his hand until I became sure he wouldn't hurt me. He never asked anything more than I could give, and for me that was very different to anything else I had experienced. We became engaged a couple of years after that and then married. My fun-loving, gentle, steady husband became a safe place, a kind of home, a place to return from my chaos and craziness. It took a while to really trust him. And it took a while for him to trust me, after he had been left so hurt from a previous relationship. But trust we did.

When I hit a low, low place, brought on by finding out we wouldn't be able to have children naturally, after years of trying, it was him who cared for me, even though he too was in pain. I felt that I had failed to provide us with a family. It felt like the world was rejecting me. It felt like my own body was rejecting me. The excitement of pre-pregnancy, when my work friends were all thinking about, or actively trying for babies too, made me an automatic part of a club – I belonged. But then months turned into years, and the people around me were on to their second babies, while we were still waiting for tests to see why we hadn't conceived. And then came the awful initial tests that showed there were problems on both sides. We'd spent years futilely trying when our chances were so low; it felt like embarrassment. I felt embarrassed that I had tried to join a club that wasn't meant for me, and I got depressed.

Around this time, we moved house. We'd been living in a Victorian terrace in Scarborough that faced straight onto the sand-coloured bricks of other terrace houses. I felt claustrophobic not being able to see green – trees, grass – and hear birds other than seagulls. I wanted to break out and escape the bricks. I kept imagining myself deep in cow parsley, surrounded by blackbird song. We took what little money we could and applied for a mortgage and got it. We found our ex-council-house paradise, a terrace with a big back garden in a tiny village, and never looked back. I began to write, waking to the peace of village life – the sound of horses in the stables, tractors rumbling by, swifts flying over the rooftops – and while we didn't live in the posh part of the village, and we didn't live in a *Country Life* house, it was utter bliss. I could walk out of my front door and up to the fields and see the ghost lake, the hummock of Seamer Beacon and, a little further out, Star Carr. I was home.

This was where the idea came to me that perhaps I could be a writer, properly, not as a hobby, but as a job. At first, I said it shyly to myself, didn't speak it out loud, simply let the idea sit in my head like a hibernating toad. I began to join online writing groups and initially took an 'introduction to poetry' course with the Open University. I built up courage by asking for feedback and learned how to analyse poetry by giving feedback in return. In the local library, I sought out poetry books.

The first poem of mine that got published was about my grandad, about his hands and how, when he died, I wanted to feel the creases in his hands again, how I could imagine the corn growing up to them, how I could imagine him on the farm where my dad was raised. It was published in a long-standing print magazine called *Acumen*. While I'm sure I would have continued writing, as I always had done ever since I was a child, I'm not sure I would have pushed myself towards a career as a writer if I hadn't gained validation from what I deemed to be the professional writing community for a poem that was about my world and my landscape.

I did an Open University BA in English Literature next, and I set myself goals – competition wins, pamphlets, a full collection – meeting each one, to my surprise. Then an MA in Creative Writing, and another pamphlet and another collection. While my writing career grew, my hopes of having a family faded. The online degrees gave me structure while my life became almost unbearable. I stuck to it, handing in an assignment days after my daughter had died. A year or so later, I attended an Open University exam while having a miscarriage. It wasn't that I was driven or determined, it was that I had a pathway – a series of steps I could take to get me where I wanted to go and, as long as I just kept taking those small steps, I would reach that destination.

After the PhD failure, I was in freefall, with no structure to my career progression. It took a long time, years, to not think of myself as a failure for having to drop out. I had to work at it, shutting down the critical voice in my head and instead asking myself what I *really* wanted, not what I thought I should be doing to fit in. I had to work at trusting my own sense of direction and my own talent. I had to learn to trust that my voice was valid, that my existence mattered as much as anyone else's.

Working with people from non-traditional writing backgrounds, founding *Spelt* magazine and building that community of writers passionate about the landscape, I began to realize that in many ways I was a 'nature writer'. The term is so loaded and has so many connotations, but I felt that being connected to the landscape in a very ordinary, everyday manner had seeped into all my work. The imagery, metaphors, similes of nature were the ones I reached for first. I'd imagined that a nature writer had to be a conqueror, but here I was existing, writing, and the world I wrote about was my own world. There are others, like me, who feel the landscape in what they create. I feel a kinship towards them.

When I arrive to interview Lindsey Tyson, she is standing in front of the paintings in the entrance hall of Woodend Galleries in Scarborough. She must have looked at them a thousand times but there she is caught in the moment, examining some fleck or sweep of paint. We've met before, what feels like a long time ago, in the pre-pandemic days when we were both working on Anne-Brontë-related projects. She's petite, swamped by a big grey jumper which makes her look as warm and welcoming as she is. We proceed through the old building, under the portrait of Edith Sitwell, whose birth home this building was. Edith stares down at us with inscrutable black eyes as we move into the basement, where Lindsey's studio is, its big double doors opening straight onto the garden.

There's been a change since I was last here, when Lindsey was focused on her textile art, beautiful felted pebbles. Lindsey developed a special printing technique allowing her to print birds, grasses and delicate landscapes on them. The studio feels different. The white walls are covered in abstract and semi-abstract paintings in deep slatey blues and peaty browns. Some of the canvases are enormous, taking up almost half the wall. I'm drawn to one in the corner, a deep brown painting, with something catching the light, moving across it from a golden corner, a shape illuminated in bronze.

I think it is a painting of a woman diving into a peat-rich loch or lake, the shape of her body just catching the sun. I make a point to ask Lindsey about it later.

Lindsey is preparing for an exhibition and has price tags on her canvases and framed pictures, and on her bowls of textile pebbles and handmade sketch pads which sit alongside the big dramatic canvases. She's in the awkward career stage of transitioning into a new way of working, trying to establish herself with a new crowd of art appreciators and buyers. It's tough in the arts. She's trying to win gallery space in well-established galleries, but to do that, she must expend thousands of pounds paying for spaces at art shows. I feel like I know this story. It is reflected in the way that the world of writing works. To be able to write well, a writer needs time and space to work on the writing, and for that they need money to live on. It feels like the art world is geared towards people who already have the money to be artists, which might explain why the arts scene is so dominated by middle-class voices, with working-class voices still on the margins.

We talk a little about the funding game, the main provider of grants being Arts Council England. We have both expended hours and hours, *weeks* of unpaid time putting applications together, bids for grassroots projects, bids for time to develop our own work, and we've both felt the sting of being unsuccessful, the frustration of not being able to claw that time back. This is how the arts world is.

Brexit has affected the way Lindsey makes textiles, and she can't buy the materials very easily anymore because the red tape around it made her suppliers stop importing or trading. In fact, they retired. Along with the pandemic and lockdowns, it was the catalyst that pushed her towards trying something new.

She says: 'I got an emergency grant because I was a small business. It meant that the pressure was off. During the pandemic I could work at the studio because I was just on my own here. I didn't have to make sales. I got a bunch of orders for the textiles and used all my materials up on those, but then I couldn't get more materials so I couldn't produce more. Instead, I took the time in my studio. I'd always wanted to try abstract stuff, but it's like starting a new career.'

The garden doors are open, and I can smell something heady from the house gardens, maybe roses. There is a real sense of a person working artistically in the space, it feels *inhabited*. I hope that my office feels like this, as if someone is here, existing, creating in the space. While the space is very still and peaceful, the paintings are full of movement. It is the movement of nature. Some of them are obviously landscapes – I can see the clouds and the wind rolling over sweeps of colour that somehow my brain automatically recognizes as moorland. I ask Lindsey what she is trying to capture in her paintings.

'It's about conveying the energy of the place, I suppose. I grew up in the countryside. I grew up playing outdoors in fields. I've always wanted to capture the energy of the sea and the energy of the wild winds and the rain. I remember being blown by the wind and being able to lean into it as a kid. You lean into it and it's holding you up. I love the elements. A lot of my paintings are quite dark, and I think people often see that as a negative, but I love it. I love the contrast between dark and light.'

We talk a little about what home means. Lindsey worked abroad; she describes herself as 'a bit of a nomad', travelling the world doing all sorts of creative jobs.

'I was trying to find my place and my place was here all the time.'

Like me, she had been put off a career in the arts by parents who wanted her to have a career that was more secure. She went back to college at the age of twenty-seven. I want to know what her relationship is to the landscape, but it's all here in the paintings. 'If you lived somewhere else, do you think you would connect to the landscape in the same way?' I ask her, between sips of tea. I can hear the seagulls gliding over the garden, and the breeze is just lifting through the doors, making itself known.

'I went to Cornwall on a residency a couple of years ago and it was lovely. It was absolutely amazing, the colours and everything, but I found it difficult to use the landscape as inspiration.'

She has, however, worked extensively with the landscape around Haworth, the moors that the Brontës walked, so what was the difference?

'There's something about the energy in Haworth that I really like as well. I'm not really a bleak moors sort of person, but there's something about the clouds – they get really big up there and the views are huge. You can just walk about and sit on a bench and the grasses are blowing in the wind around you. In Scarborough it is the sea's energy I try to capture. But it's the weather, the elements, that I love, and how you are just amongst it – it's just so powerful. When the winds are so strong, and the rain pours in, it makes you feel alive. I like a nice sunny day too, but it doesn't make me want to paint.'

We stand to look at the canvases. She points out the semi abstracts and the abstracts and tells me about the different audiences and how she wants to get more buyers for the abstracts, but they are harder to sell. I'm intrigued by the differences between visual art and literature, whether there's a difference in what we want the reader, or the observer, to take away. 'What do you want the art appreciator, the observer to understand about your art?' I ask.

'I want them to respond to the art. But also, I want them to know the value of it, the skill and the work that has gone into it.'

We talk a little more about the similarities between painting and writing and the building of skill over time. But mostly we talk about the landscape and our connection to it. How we feel when we paint a landscape, an abstract landscape, or write a poem that involves the landscape. We are trying to capture the characteristics – I say the *personality* – of the place.

I think my own work is about burrowing down and trying to find foundations. I realize that, for a long time, I have been trying to validate myself as an artist. Lindsey's shared experience of building a career and finding a way to do the art that feels right for her strikes a simple, healing bell in my mind. This is what I want, to be me, being me, creating art of the things that interest me, not necessarily the things that validate me as an artist. This too feels a little like coming home, like a personal journey marker on my route to belonging and self-acceptance. Before I go, I ask Lindsey about the painting in the corner, the peat lake, the woman diving.

'It was winter and I was walking by the spa. Some film crew had been making a film down there and the spotlight was still shining on the sea. It was quite a woolly night, and I just . . . I painted the electricity, coming out like lightning, the energy of the sky coming down to the energy of the sea.'

What does it say about me, I wonder as I'm making my way back out of town to the car park, that in that

217

picture I saw a woman diving into the murk of a peat-filled lake?

Often working-class rural artists are seen as quaint or 'rustic' – a devaluation of the creative practice. Whereas the observed act of nature writing, or visual art featuring nature, from people visiting the countryside and reporting back to an urban audience – especially by people who might be deemed as middle class or with a higher educational background to the artists and writers living and working in a rural setting – is often seen to have more value than the work produced *by* people living the rural life, especially those from working-class backgrounds. You only have to walk into a high street bookshop to see that there is a trend in rural writing that is skewed towards stories of people who have moved from urban to rural settings – middle-class people who have left soul-crushing metropolitan jobs for a 'simple rural lifestyle'. This in turn reduces the representation of rural working-class writers, both physically by providing less space on the shelves, and by allowing a stereotype of rural arts to continue that makes it harder for working-class people to get a foot in the door because they are constantly thought of as 'other than the norm'. It makes the stories of working-class writers – their own true stories, their perspectives on the world – less valuable than those stories of reinvention, because it pushes them further into the background. There is limited space for writers, there are limited opportunities for writers, and if you are already on the back foot trying to find space, if you are already having to kick down doors because you are not seen as the correct 'fit' for the industry, it galls to see yet another version of *Escape to the Country* on the shelves.

How much are rural working-class stereotypes internalized by rural working-class artists? If you are only ever seen as, only ever recognize yourself as, a background figure in a painting by a middle-class painter, how do you know that you too can be the painter observing the scene? If you are only ever the well-meaning country folk described by someone moving to a village and finding that the buses don't run past 7 p.m., how will you ever know that you could be talking about the buses, about the darkness, about other, bigger issues, about love, about anger, about relationships. If the work you create is seen as rustic, less than, devalued as a perspective, if our voices are devalued it is more difficult to fit into a world that doesn't speak our language, where our accents still stand out.

Admission to the arts world is built on an assumption that everybody knows how to access it and can access it. It relies on an understanding of the language of grant applications, and a university education. This is still the language of accent correction, this is still the language of gatekeeping. It places the effort squarely on the working-class artist who must learn the language, learn the skills, learn the methodology, court the contacts to enter. The perspective is still one in which we need to better ourselves, work on ourselves, change ourselves, if we want to be admitted. We need pathways and opportunities open to us so that our stories are as valued and valid as anyone else's in the arts. We need the doors open so *we* too can tell our stories.

My story isn't extraordinary or exceptional. Although I've had my battles, I have not had to fight every day just to stay alive. I have not conquered anything, except my own low self-esteem, and even that isn't conquered, it is simply accepted and understood. But my voice and my story are valid. I would like to be a working-class writer writing about something other than being a working-class writer. And I will be.

I think again about Lindsey, and the push that helped her to find the space just to do what she wanted to do. The push was a pandemic, distance, money to survive and thrive. Perhaps I still do not value my own work and am constantly trying to justify the place that I am taking at the table. I want just to stop and create.

I'm in my office. It is the room that would have been a children's bedroom, but I have converted it to the *room of my own* to write in. It is mid-June, but a cloud bank has sat for over a week down the eastern side of the country, and it is still quite chilly. I have yet to take my winter duvet off.

Earlier I walked the elderly dog up to the field of oilseed rape and down a little tufted strip of unworked farmland. I saw a great sleek hare and her leveret. I greeted her quietly, as if she was the daughter I lost, because all hares are my daughter in a way I can't explain. I have not visited my daughter's grave for a while. Instead I find her out here. All the world, all the landscape, has folded itself around me, and I have reached for its comfort here.

June is a glorious month for walking, for being outside. But this year June has a different feel to it. We are approaching my dad's birthday, right next door to Father's Day, and the adverts on TV are a constant reminder that he is gone. I had forgotten this pain, of the world moving on. We were never a family who demonstrated emotions easily. We are not huggers. And there was always a slight awkwardness around Father's Day and birthdays, though my dad was ever joyous with whatever gift he was given. I realize I miss the ritualistic nudge to let him know that he is loved. Often I find myself, after all these months, on the verge of tears when I remember that those yearly opportunities are gone. Of course, I know that he knew we loved him. But perhaps the thing that I miss is the opportunity to remind myself that I am part of that family unit.

My mind keeps coming back to a moment in the room next to the Intensive Therapy Unit, the quiet space which had been set up with biscuits, tea, juice and comfortable chairs. The room allowed us to pass into a version of normality after watching Dad's controlled death in front of us. It was, in fact, minutes after we had been told that his heart had stopped. After the agonizing fifteen minutes following life support being switched off and Dad slowing to a stop like a wound-down toy. There was relief in reaching the oasis of the quiet room and relief in knowing that this, or this part, was over. We had been a family of five just minutes before, and now we were a family of four. The terrible maths of it. Five minus one equals four. The certainty of being a number in the five-pointed unit of my family suddenly gone. Then we walked past all the other beds in the ITU with their sleeping patients and musical bleeps and soft alarms and the families clasping hands, the shy looks towards us, at the ones who hadn't made it, and then we were out into the sudden surprise of a hot summer's day.

My sister and I stood waiting while my brother helped my mum collect herself and, as we did, two dragonflies blew up from nowhere, circling each other in a whirlwind of glittering blue. They were the colour of the sea as seen on holiday for the first time, bright and sparkling, and they swirled around our faces and then separated and flew away over the hospital car park. I reached for this sudden vision of natural beauty and thought of my dad, his energy, his vitality and how this was a symbol – my parents as dragonflies, separating, the beautiful flying away to somewhere we did not know.

My dad wanted to be buried on the land he'd worked so hard to own. In the weeks that followed we forced our way through all the red tape and admin that burying someone on your own land takes. It turns out burying a whole human is very, very complicated and involves measuring distances to water courses and alerting the police to the fact there will be a body in your garden so that in future they know it isn't a murder victim. Then one day I went to see my mum and she told me she'd found a dead tawny owl in the field where Dad was to be buried. So unusual. So strange. My mind reached towards angry spirits – was Dad unhappy that we weren't managing to carry out his death wishes? At that point, we were on the cusp of giving in, the complexity of getting him buried the way he wanted was exhausting. He had been very specific – wicker coffin, hay beneath him, buried fully in the field he owned, going back to the earth. We were talking then of having him cremated, so that we could scatter his ashes, or even bury his ashes.

Something about the dead owl willed us on. It was a sign. We saw what needed to be done. For months afterwards, my mum would comment on a tawny owl she could hear calling from the bottom of the field, and she'd say it was Dad calling to her. Eventually, we found our way through, we propped each other up, each of us taking responsibility for the part of funeral planning that suited us best. In the end, the burial was a beautiful thing – the oaks were full of acorns that dropped around his grave, the breeze blew, and it was as peaceful and special as he would have wanted it to be. We were able to bury him in the field on our land, as he had wished.

There were other times when we reached for signs in nature to help us deal with grief, for messages my dad might be leaving. One day my mum was struggling with Dad's fishpond, a pond that he had built himself and therefore was full of special knacks and methods to keep it running, tricks that only he knew. She couldn't find the source of a leak behind the rockery. It was at a time when she was feeling particularly overwhelmed with the small-holding and a need to carry on my dad's legacy, as the custodian of his life. Instead of the leak, she found a patch of bright yellow cowslips. It was as if he'd sent her a gift.

# CHAPTER TWELVE

# The Crossgates Boulder

We are heading into the still and sweltering days of midsummer, and the heat has hit hot and fierce. The elderly dog and I walk the lanes around the village, moving from one shady spot to another. I can already hear a decrease in birdsong as more energy is put into raising broods than finding mates. Today's pilgrimage is to the other end of the lake site and the housing estate where I grew up. I want to visit a boulder there. It's an erratic boulder – a boulder carried by a glacier and deposited far away from its original home, which geologists think was in Cumbria. But first the elderly dog needs his walk, and the middle-aged woman needs her walk. This is the everyday connection to nature and place that I seek – a simple act – a slow walk down the lane, the old dog at my side.

I'm watching the cycle of life played out around me. As we pass under a big willow, I can hear a fledgling crow calling and the parent answering from an old hawthorn hedge grown into a tree line. I wait beneath the boughs, the dog nearby, panting in the shade. Sure enough, in comes the parent, calling that guttural rasp, the fledgling replying, the noise growing in intensity until the parent pushes its beak far into the fledgling's gullet to feed it – an almost violent act of care, of nourishment, before it is off again in a clatter of wings. We walk on. What do I want from the boulder visit today? I want something that is difficult to put into words. I want to feel its stillness, its permanence within a changing landscape.

The lane feels like it is full of the drama of survival. I watch as six swallows chase the slender brown shape of a kestrel away from their nesting sites, and then a buzzard is harried away by jackdaws. Even a squirrel, crossing from one side of the road to the other, meets the anger of nesting house martins who dive at it until it picks up speed and launches itself onto a tree, provoking angry croaks from nearby magpies.

We make it to the top field, following a narrow path with bushels of cow parsley and thick nettles on either side. There are horses nearby, placidly tearing at the long grasses. The field of oilseed rape is no longer yellow, no longer flowering, but a whole swathe of waist-high green stalks, the pods bubbling with seeds. There is no shade here, but I can see that where the path turns down towards Lingholme Farm, the trees lining it cast a dark shadow where the sun won't have reached yet. I chivvy the old dog along, trying to get him through this patch of heat to the next block of relief. When we get there, I stop, and after a few minutes the dog lies down to rest in the still-dewy grass.

I am on top of a slight rise in the landscape, a slope down towards the valley floor where I can look towards Folkton and Flixton. I am between the sea and the lake site. This is where I have ended up, washed to the edges by everything that has come before me. I feel a deep sense of connection to this place, but really that connection is to the history of this place and not necessarily to the living, working landscape that is the lake site now, in 2023. There is a part of me that worries that I have romanticized this place. After all, it is easier to write the stories of people who can't rewrite them. Perhaps there is an element of control in this, that remedies the lack of control I have felt in my own life, the way I seem to have washed chaotically along like leaf litter in a rainstorm, never quite knowing who I was or where I fitted in.

I leave the dog sleeping on the sofa and drive down to Crossgates, pulling the car into Station Road. I grew up in Crossgates, a semi-rural place of box-like houses backing onto open fields, though the fields are not so open now. In a pattern that is repeating itself across the country, new houses are appearing, villages are expanding, estates are merging into each other. I find myself thinking of the clichéd line *This used to all be fields*. I stop and really look at the place, for the first time in years. I'm standing near to the 'new' houses that I watched being built when I lived here in the 1990s. As children, my brother, sister and I would spend time in the remnants of a burned-down farm-house, feeling for the old kitchen flags in the sandy soil. We played in the crumbling ruins, where a range still stood, slanted, and leaning back into the ground. We found pots and pans and tokens of a life lived there that meant nothing to us. I don't remember it burning down, I don't remember what came before the scratchy ruins that were our play-ground, or if anyone died there. The burned-down farmhouse is gone now, replaced by a lovely park area and nicely presented housing estate, a set of small shops and a community centre. This is a kind of life cycle too. Where once I sat in the window of the boxroom in my childhood home and looked out over the fields to the railway line and the quarry, now the view is only houses, houses, houses. In this place, the semi-rural is being eaten by the urban, or at least the sub-urban.

The boulder sits on the corner of the road that peels off the bypass down to the station. It has a plaque beneath it which tells visitors that it is important, not just a boulder but a Shap granite boulder, a kind of rock that is not local to the area. Why is it important? Because it tells us how the ice flow, the glacier that created this valley, moved. This boulder was carried in its belly as it ground the valley into existence, and then deposited here, or rather deposited in the garden of the station house and moved here in the 1980s. It's a sizeable thing – six foot high and six foot in diameter, at least. It sat for thousands of years in the well of the valley, was there before the Palaeolithic people of Flixton Island, before the Mesolithic people of Star Carr, before Carman's Spital. While life has moved on around it, it has remained completely still within the landscape. As a child I saw it moved to this position when they were widening the road. They transported it in a sling, by crane. It's such a hazy memory. I was nine, but I remember the way the weight of it kept the fabric of the sling taut. I imagine a person could count on one hand the number of times the boulder has moved. I want to anthropomorphize it. My natural tendency is to call it peaceful, at rest, a sentinel, a watcher. It has provided a steadiness to my life. Especially here in Crossgates.

I go to the boulder and lay my hands on it and feel its

crags and fissures, see up close its rough surface. It is a beautiful boulder. The rock is a sandy yellow-pink and there are sparkling crystals embedded in it. It is just a rock, but it does not feel ordinary. The boulder sits opposite a bus shelter. I passed by as a child, as a teen, as an adult. I am still passing by it now. When I try to express what I think about this thing, this inanimate object that is a part of my life, it is something to do with the unstoppable passage of time. It is something about time going so fast – the human life like a sparrow in a mead hall – but also so slowly that a stone can stand still for thousands of years. I imagine the sound of the glacier creaking and carving into the ground. This boulder speaks to me about my own mortality.

When my dad died, I became much more aware of my own mortality. I felt as if I was both the boulder that had arrived during the creation of this place, and a mote, a blink of the eyes, a nothing passing through the landscape. I felt fragile and eternal at once.

I worry about wasting the time I have left on the planet, and what the right thing to do with that time might be. This thought didn't come up after I lost my daughter. That loss was like a blinding white light that burned me, something terrible that shouldn't have happened. That loss made me wild. I became aware of myself as an animal, a thing of impulse and teeth and emotion. It returned me to an authentic self that I had forgotten existed. In a way, I liked the authenticity that grief gave me, and the ability to see civilized society was just a construct, that really, we were still, all of us, primal animals doing our best to survive.

My dad's death was terrible, traumatic, but a loss I knew I would face sooner or later. Through the loss of my dad, I became aware of my ancestry, my place in the line, as if he had always been a link in a chain, and that I had always been safely linked to my ancestry through him. When that link was removed, it drove me to make new links. It made me aware of myself within the context of the world, and aware of my mortal body in a way I wasn't before. When we buried him in the field behind my parents' house, I had a sense of a mask being lifted, the rules of society breaking down, the sort of transcendence that one experiences when something out of the ordinary occurs. And I realized that my dad had a real connection to land, and that from him I had inherited this connection, but I had also lived it in my own way.

I realized there is very little time in a human life. If we are lucky, we might experience eighty years on this planet, and I am here at forty-six, more than halfway through. My daughter's death taught me that the worst thing could happen, and to waste my time would be to disregard the time that she had not had. My dad's death taught me that time is very, very finite, and that we are part of the cruellest trick – an intelligent organism that knows its own fate. How can we live with that knowledge? I don't know the answer. I don't know why we aren't driven mad with the knowing of it. I imagine this is why we are hard-wired to seek meaning in everything, and where there is none, to create meaning.

It feels like loss has brought me to this place and has left me with this precious gift – life. I want to be brave. I want to follow my own path. I want to say, *One way to make the most of your precious life is simply to exist in it.* To make room to walk and think. To write but write not to conquer the world, but simply to explore. I want to tell myself that I don't have to solve the world's problems. This is enough. But the voice that says all this stuff, things that I truly believe in my heart, is very quiet, very far away. It is the voice from my childhood. It is the voice of a working-class kid who left school at sixteen. What would she know about life?

In the years after my daughter died, it seemed essential that I should run marathons to raise money for charity, that I should write articles about infant mortality and speak on television and radio about problems in the NHS. I raged against a society that dismissed women's sense of their own bodies, a medical system that dismissed you if the word 'anxious' or 'anxiety' appeared on your records, how that led to things being overlooked.

My mind would always come back to that hospital room, the spinning fan, the unseasonable heat, the way I felt like an animal in a cage that wanted, desperately, to break free. I wanted this never to happen to anyone else ever again. But it did keep happening. It does keep happening. I am further and further away from the day I woke up on the hospital bed and they told me my baby had died. I feel relieved, and a little guilty, letting the fight that would never have a resolution go. I see other women who have been through similar experiences, ten years younger than me, twenty years younger than me, going through the same process, gradually becoming distanced, gradually washing up at the edges of their own lives searching for purpose and a sense of identity. I guess this is what I am doing now, as I track my own trail along the shores of the ghost lake. I am making my own paths, I am making my own connections, I am creating a sense of belonging in myself that is not reliant on other

people, a sense of belonging that means that I can just
*be*.

On the summer solstice, a day before my dad's birthday,
I reach for ritual again. I want to make the effort to be
present for something, something just for myself. I decide
to watch the sunrise on the beach at Filey. This is something
I have often thought about doing but have never actually
done. Perhaps I feel I have been too busy, or it seems too
strange, an odd thing to do – to go to watch the sun rise
in the hope of feeling something spiritual – or maybe it is
just an odd thing to go alone, or maybe it is not odd at
all, and I simply worry about being perceived as odd, no
matter what I do. I decide to embrace the oddness, embrace
myself, and let my odd self lead.

I wake at 4 a.m. and it is already getting light. I wonder
if I can muster the energy, though I am already alert, and
I know that it is the discomfort of doing something new
that bothers me. I don't stop to think. I get up, get dressed,
grab a notebook and pen from my writing room, my phone,
my bag and stride down through the dewy garden to the
car. I drive on the silent roads where only one or two other
vehicles are about.

The wild world has already begun its day some time
ago. The birds seem slow and sleepy, the deer in the fields
unbothered by my presence. The heavy rain has bent the
wheat fields, the grasses lie wan and defeated in the thin
light. Then down the cobbled slope to the beach, through
the trees where the blackbirds are singing, singing, singing.
I remember a time a couple of summers back when I was
in the habit of riding my push bike down here on mornings

like this. A habit I put aside because it took me away from planning and prepping and organizing my life. I make a mental note to build this practice back into my routine.

I park up on the promenade. The air is already warm with summer. There are two people silhouetted against the sky on the rocky outcrop of Carr Naze – two tiny stick people far away. There are also two motorcyclists standing at the railing, as well as a lady on the beach and a man walking, who stops to ask me if I am there for the solstice. We are all there to witness it, each of us creating our own private ritual to the rising sun, far removed from Stonehenge and the deep passageways of Neolithic temples. In the sea a group of paddleboarders bob in the ripples, seal-like. I imagine the way they might almost reach out to touch the sun. A salmon fishing boat putts into view, and far out, on the horizon, a container ship.

The sky is already pinkish orange when I arrive, but there is no visible sun yet. The air is full of the sea and the sound of gulls. I take big breaths, lungfuls, great buckets of the rich sea air, and I feel like I might cry at the purity of the moment, that I have come down to the beach and done the thing I always said I would do – a simple miracle of witnessing light. But it is not simple, not to me.

I give myself a pat on the back, a recognition of the small acts of strength it takes to be the person I am, to accept that I will always be on the edges, and to embrace that, to recognize that the thing that makes me stick out, not fit in, has led to a rich internal life, one I would not swap. I am restless to start with, unsure how to hold my body or how to sit on the bench, and wondering who might be watching from the windows of the many beautiful buildings and apartments. I feel self-conscious, but I am there to do this thing, on my own terms. There is nothing to do but wait for this great thing to happen, this beginning of the longest day, this turning point. I want it to be a turning point for me, too. I worry that the sunrise won't be as beautiful as I have imagined. I needn't have worried.

First, the tiny bright spot on the crag of Carr Naze. Then slowly, but somehow not slowly, the sun rises; unstoppable, enormous, a great eye of gold, bright gold, so bright I have to turn away, as if I am looking at the face of God. A finger of pure gold lays itself across the sea directly to my feet like a miracle, like I have been chosen. The sea chops the light into a leaf-fall of gold, but then it becomes solid again, as the sun rises and casts away the filamentous clouds, and the little boat catches the light, and the caravans on the hill are blessed by the sun on their windows which turns everything gilded and rich and precious.

I think about the Neolithic folk, with their burial chambers and passage tombs, aligned to the solstice. I have watched the summer solstice streamed live from Newgrange in Ireland, a huge, domed stone tomb covered in Neolithic artwork like that found on the Folkton Drums. I have watched the sun creep down the passage to touch the back wall of the tomb and wondered about the rituals and the meaning behind them; how the sliver of light must have rested on the feet of the people in the tomb, how they might have felt the way I do; that it might have made them feel special, touched by nature. I wait for the sun to settle into the sky and then return to my quiet car, driving through the sleeping town, through the empty streets, the shops silently admitting the light of this new sun into their windows.

At home the chickens are up and waiting for their corn. A snail is making its slow way up the lawn. The cat greets me warmly. I percolate coffee and look in at my sleeping husband, soft and beautiful, and the elderly dog fast asleep in his bed, and my office, full of sunlight and the birdsong from the garden. I settle myself at my desk to write.

As the day comes to life, I watch friends on social media seeing in the solstice in their own ways. My plan is to drive out to the ghost lake, to stand on the bridge and look down the crease of the valley and watch the sun setting that same day, to imagine the Star Carr people doing the same, and the Neolithic people just over the brow ridge on Folkton Wold, and the Bronze Age people over at Seamer Beacon. This is my plan. But what actually happens is that my husband suggests a drive to Filey, a pint in our favourite pub, a Chinese takeaway, and we do this instead, eating with the windows open and the swifts screeching down the village. Later I take the elderly dog for a late evening walk and witness the sun setting over the village roofs. This too feels like a ritual. A ritual feast, a ritual of home and hearth and love and connection.

# CHAPTER THIRTEEN

# Seamer

I've been given permission to metal detect on a small-holding in the next village along from my own. Metal detecting is one of those things that I always wanted to do but had never dared to until recently. Something about being observed, being looked at, being perceived, thought nerdy or *weird*, put me off. Overcoming my shyness, having the courage to approach people and ask to work on their land was another small challenge to navigate. Being an object of curiosity for passing cars, having people ask me the question *Found anything?* or *Found any gold?* repeatedly, has started to lose its strangeness. So far, I've been lucky and have landed a few permissions with land-owners whose love for the place is evident in their interest in what I have found.

It is midsummer. Some days it's so hot and dry I can barely get the spade into the ground. But today is fresh, a cool breeze is blowing down from the east, from the sea, carrying the scent of seaweed and rock pools. There has been some rain over the last few days, enough to make the ground give.

I arrive and pull the car onto the gravel of the forecourt. Richard, the owner of the farm, is waiting for me, ready to show me around. He shows me the fields I can go in and the fields that are off limits. He shows me where the swallows have been nesting in the barn. We stand still, surrounded by bales of hay and quietly chewing horses, watching the birds flit about. There is a delicious horsey smell, of dung and leather. I have a sudden urge to climb up onto the hay bales and go to sleep. Then he shows me the best place to see the hares that are always, he says, in the field in the corner, and where the fox comes through the gap in the fence, and where he says he lost a piece of his hay-baling machine and how happy he would be if I found it for him – apparently it's an expensive part. I never do find it.

Later in the day, when I shear off the edge of my trowel on a hawthorn root, he sharpens it for me on a lathe in his workshop. He is excited to tell me about the land, about how long he has been here and what he has found out about its history. Before I arrive, I look up old maps of the area and research when the railway line was built. The trains pass every hour, along one side of the field. I get used to seeing the same train driver go backwards and forwards, the craned necks of the passengers. Sometimes, when the train passes, I am digging, sometimes walking, sometimes near the track, sometimes far away. I picture myself as the driver must see me, a selection of panels, a story of myself, in which I am always doing something slightly different, always with my head down, listening to the land. Richard waves to me as he is going about his business and I wave back as I am going about mine, but apart from that, I am left to my own devices for hours at a time.

The first thing I do, once I have checked I have everything I need, is to say a silent thank you to the land, for allowing me to work on it. I ask it to tell me its stories and release the past to me so that I can handle it and know this place. Then I ground the detector, put my headphones on and begin the slow, methodical, mindful stitching of the land, listening to the bleeps and whistles as I sweep left and right, keeping the coil as flat as I can to the surface.

It's a good field. There are patches where stuff has been burned. These are a nightmare for metal detectors, nothing but grey sooty wells of melted nails and drawer handles. But otherwise, the field is quiet, with very little interference. When I do get a good signal, it is usually something interesting. That day I strike gold, literally. A solid gold Victorian sovereign. The first and only gold I have ever found. I take it to show Richard who beams ear to ear. Later I'll have it valued and, because I want to keep it in my collection, we agree that I will give him half its worth. Richard tells me weeks later that it paid for him to take his children and grandchildren out for the day, and how nice it was to have spare cash just to enjoy a day out without worrying about it.

Over the course of a week, I move across the field. I find a button that has a shop name printed on it. I research the shop – a high-end Victorian equine livery specialist in Scarborough, long gone now – and show Richard pictures of it. It's worth nothing, but we both enjoy the link between an equestrian rider passing through the field and losing a button, and Richard's daughter riding her horse on this land. The landscape is a kind of connective tissue between eras.

On the last day of metal detecting at the smallholding, I notice hares in the bottom corner of the field. I move towards them, sweeping my way quietly and methodically in that direction. One hare runs, but the other stays pinned under the fence. I wonder what it's doing, until it springs from the field and runs almost over my feet and away. *It must have a leveret nearby*, I think, and as the words are forming in my mind, the coil of the detector sweeps over a fawn-coloured form, lying still as a rock in the grass. I start moving slowly backwards and away, trying not to disturb it, but it is already disturbed, and runs across the field and away through the hawthorn hedge. I bend and touch the place where it has been, laying my palm flat on the bent grass. I can feel the warmth of its body. Someone in one of the online metal detecting groups I'm part of once told me to look for the animals when I was detecting, as they are often where good finds are, which sounds ridiculous, but when I turn the earth over at that spot, out of the ground comes part of a key, a very old key. I look it up later in my finds book and see that it is probably Tudor. I hold it up to the light. It looks like the shaft has snapped in use. The hare showed me where the key was, and when I dug, I found it.

It's been a while since I visited my daughter's grave, not since early spring when the trees were bare and the ground muddy and frozen. I arrive, in the middle of summer, on a day of low, black-blue clouds, when the air is thick with the pressure of an incoming thunderstorm. It is the sort of day that stagnates your body. I feel limp and tired just thinking about going anywhere and doing anything. But the idea of her grave being neglected has been nibbling away at me and, even though I have long since unburdened myself of the idea of regular grave visits, I still want her to know she is loved. I park up and sit for a moment, windows down, listening to the way the wind moves through the mature trees. It is instantly soothing, the way that only sensory experiences soothe me.

The cemetery feels alive with the summer, everything green and shady. I can hear the distant sound of sheep bleating. They sound insistent, perhaps a little desperate, and I wonder if this is the weaning time, and these are the mothers calling for their young, and the young perhaps calling back. In a few days they'll stop calling, mostly, and will continue their sheep lives. Do they simply forget that their children existed? Or do they simply accept that their children are not with them anymore, that they have gone on to be mothers themselves, or gone on to be fattened up for meat?

I look at the white marble and gold lettering of my daughter's grave, and I think about the way in which I have accepted that she isn't with me and while it took years, and for years I called and called for her, she was not coming back. I was calling for her all through the IVFs that followed, and I was calling for her all through the investigation into her death, and she was never coming back. I loved her in a way that is hard to describe. I think that my body loved her, and my soul loved her, and when she was separated from me, I didn't know how to exist. I think that when I was with her, I had a specific identity, and when I was without her, I went back to not knowing who I was. I think it took me a long time to stop calling for her, and I do not think that that is wrong. It took the time it was meant to take. Some of that time was spent waiting for the glacier to carve new territory in the land-scape of myself, sometimes I was draining the land to make progress, sometimes I was hunting in the marshes, sometimes I was the marsh swallowing people whole.

After I finish tidying the grave and refilling the water in the vases, cutting peonies the colour of strawberries and roses the colour of lemons, I stop to feel the cemetery around me. It never feels like a place of death to me. Rather, it feels like a place of life coexisting with death, as if the two aren't really that separate. I will never know if my daughter knew me, or if she felt any pain or fear. All those questions, those heavy, unbearable questions, will go unanswered. I think I have come to terms with that.

The breeze is shifting the leaves of the trees in a constant murmur. A squirrel is moving through the leaf litter. I feel like I have been on one of my hikes and ended up in this place, and that pleases me. I stand to face the hillside behind me, the ridge, over which is the Bronze Age cemetery and Seamer Beacon. I can't see any of it – the angle is too steep. But I know it is there, and the link to myself and to my daughter is there, and they are not forgotten. I have tried to remember these lake ancestors. I kiss my hand to my daughter's headstone, *We love you, we miss you, you are not forgotten*, and take her memory away with me.

As I drive away and double back on the cemetery, taking a road out of town that rises above it, I take a quick glance over to the headstones and repeat my mantra *I love you, I miss you, you are not forgotten.* Then I'm passing the beacon, its shape rising then falling away as I drive over the lip of the valley and see the stretch of it in front of me.

Some days, now, are so muggy I can hardly breathe. It's on a day like this that I drive round the lake to the other side, to my parents' house in Seamer. Of course, the house is no longer my parents' house, it is now only my mum's house, my dad's legacy like a receding tide. I'm looking after Mum's chickens and keeping an eye on the property while she's on holiday again with her sisters.

The air feels so thick with heat that it seems to stir as I park up at the barn and get out of the car. This house has never held a great deal of appeal to me. I look at the amount of work it takes to keep it going and feel a kind of second-hand anxiety. But today, on a day like this when the roses are in full bloom and the substantial veg patch is brimming with produce, the fishpond tinkling, my dad's koi swimming peacefully within, yes, I can see the appeal. My dad shrank a farm down to a farm set here, carried the experiences of his youth into this more manageable place. The pond, we know, is leaking, but we're not sure where from. The level seems fine today though, so no need to top it up. I head into the barn and my father's workshop to sort out the feed for the chickens, and I see a mouse moving along the shelf at the back, slipping behind tins full of screws and nails, old baccy. My dad's workshop. A pile of sawdust at the side of the lathe. A notebook with a picture of something – a shed? And my mum's writing next to it. My dad's spidery numbers. A plan that will never now come to fruition. The clock that I remember from my childhood kitchen is stuck at ten to eleven.

The camper van takes up most of the space in here. It's another one of Dad's projects. Built on a truck chassis, it is difficult to find parts for. Just last week, as we sat by the pond drinking tea, my mum began to talk about letting it go. It has no power steering, so she'd never be able to drive it. It needs maintaining, fixing, by someone who knows what they're doing. Time for someone else to make memories in it. It marks a shift, like the solstice, turning to face a different side of the year, one where the possibility of letting some of my dad's things go becomes an idea that isn't as devastating as it was six months ago. Lately she's seemed more at peace. She talks less about not being able to stop seeing in her head the image of Dad dying, and more about the fifty years of marriage they had, how lucky they were, how lucky she was. I run my fingers along the side of the camper, along the decal that says proudly *Yorkshire Born and Bred* with a picture of the white rose of Yorkshire on the side. I hope the van goes to someone who will enjoy it.

I'm carrying the feed buckets and water and a tray for eggs through the garden past the polytunnel, where I can see the grapevine is loaded with fruit. I make a mental note to make wine this year. Perhaps it might be nice, at Christmas, to pass around Dad's variety wine. As I head towards the field, I pass the patch where raspberries are beginning to plump and startle three thieving magpies and two rabbits from among the fruit. The magpies rise in a clatter of croaks and cawing. The rabbits, just babies really, scatter in panic, first running straight towards me, then zigzagging away. I make a mental note not to tell my mother and give her more to worry about.

The chickens are all quite old now but still laying well. They are a mix of ex-battery hens and fancy breeds. They come running when I call and I count them up, notice some are missing. In the chicken shed three are scrunched low in the nesting boxes, reluctant for me to put my hand under them. Broody hens. I *do* put my hand under, facing the momentary fear of being pecked, and find nothing. No eggs. The hens huff at me, but I leave my hand beneath the black one for a little longer, feeling the soft feathers, the utter heat of her body, the warm straw, the scale of her legs. She cocks her head and looks up at me, a mixture of indignant and resigned. I let her get on with her fantasy brooding and make sure they have water and feed. I should move them, really, otherwise they will remain broody, and I hate removing eggs from broody hens.

As I turn, I see, on the perching rack, right at the back in the corner, a hen lying face down. I call and chivvy, but the hen looks dead. I can't quite reach her, so I use a broom to drag her body up the rack, disturbing hen poo and lost feathers as I do. The hens are old. They are coming towards the end of their lives. They are healthy and happy and live outside in the sunshine. They have had good lives pecking freely in the field, breathing fresh air. This hen seems to have simply died in her sleep. I would wish for a life like this, I think, of air and earth and being content.

After I've dealt with the dead chicken, I finish up feeding and watering and head round to see my dad's grave. It doesn't feel like I am seeing my dad. But then it has never felt like I was seeing my daughter, when I visit her grave at Woodlands. The grave here is marked only by a few white chalk stones and some solar lights. It has settled nicely, the grass merging in, reclaiming the land. There is the slightest rise to the earth and a vague coffin-shaped demarcation which will eventually fade. The oak tree is full and green and hangs its leaves over the grave. On the other side of the chicken fence, the chickens are grouped like a choir, come to see what it is that I am doing, whether there is anything in it for them.

I think of a photo we used in the funeral, my dad standing here, doing something with the chicken run, the chickens, his girls, all standing just like this. After all the trauma, all the terrible grief, this is the most perfect, peaceful place for my dad. I wish for this too, that I shall have this peace in the grave. I wish for my life to be bookended by this landscape, the place where I was born and, I hope, the place where I will die. The grave that I eventually go into, of course, will be Matilda's grave, my daughter's grave. We shall be added to it, under the beech trees and the copper hedges, where the deer will come picking among the headstones, eating the offerings left by those who grieve.

I finish up and drive back home. Through Seamer, past Star Carr, past Spital Farm and then turning towards the sea, past Flixton, under the rim of the Wolds, the Folkton barrows away and out of sight, into Folkton village, crossing the lake. Seamer Beacon sits proud on the horizon opposite.

I pull the car over and walk up to the bridge that spans the width of the River Hertford. This is a lush time of year. Fields and fields of wheat, the river reedy and sluggish, silvering in the sun. Two buzzards are drifting across the valley, looking down on it, seeing the whole shape of the lake site. I can work out where Star Carr is, again, from here, where Flixton Island is. The mound of the municipal tip like a modern long barrow. I can scan my eyes along the side of the lake, the opposite side, and see the chip factory puffing potato-flavoured steam into the air, and the school I attended as a teenager. If I could pass into the body of one of the buzzards, I would see all of this, a map of the land that you would only know is there if you were a part of it, aware of it. And there, on the bridge, myself within the landscape.

There is nothing of the lake here, except a watermark left in the wet ground, a mist that rises sometimes, a shroud. The lake has changed, so much, so slowly. As landscape changes, and as we change the landscape, the landscape changes us. We are dependent, still, on what the earth gives up for our use and in return, while taking from it, we change it, we change the purpose of the land, and by proxy the purpose of the land for other animals, other parts of the ecosystem.

Robert MacFarlane, describing the celebrated Scottish nature writer, novelist and poet Nan Shepherd in the introduction to her extraordinary book on walking the Cairngorm mountains, *The Living Mountain*, said of her that she was a 'localist of the best kind'. This word, 'localist', has stayed with me. Not just as an identity, but as a concept. And as a permission slip, that allows me to shrug off the idea that to know nature, to know the landscape, you must conquer it. When I came home, from the Unsuitable Man's house, from the failed PhD, from my daughter's body, born and dead in Leeds Hospital, I came back to a physical place I call home, but I also came back to a concept I call home, an identity that had something to do with roots, family, ancestry and class, but also something less definable, something about belonging, to myself, to my landscape.

All landscapes are personal. The landscape you live in is not just an archive of past lives, past geological and natural events, but an archive of your own story. I am thinking again of the glacial boulder. It has been a silent observer of the changing landscape, here from the very beginning. It is also the rock on which I had my first kiss, the bus stop opposite is where I smoked my first cigarette, the station beneath it is where I took a train away with the Unsuitable Man. I have been on a pilgrimage for over a year, looking for myself in this place, turning over my memories and reconnecting to the lineage of the land.

It is such a beautiful day that I decide to drive over to

Folkton, to walk and feel the sun on my skin. I park up and walk the steep slope of the valley towards the Folkton Drums burial site. I stop to sit on the bench memorializing the COVID pandemic frontline workers. For a while, I close my eyes and listen to the breeze in the grass and in the trees further down. The bench is hot, heated by the sun. I let the light play on the lids of my eyes, making the world red. I stretch and feel the gorse, encroaching on my seat, the spiky grass on the other side, the chalky earth beneath. I can smell the homely, comforting smell of cows and sheep. When I open my eyes, it is to the lake site, all of it. I am level with the beacon now, proud, prominent on the other side of the valley. I can see my own village, the place I have landed. The place with my husband and my animals where I have washed up and rooted.

The lake site has been changing for thousands of years. Even in the blink of my own life, the landscape has changed, the earth buckling, drying, the newbuilds spreading across the surrounding land, but still I can imagine the water of it, the trees, the wolves, the Star Carr people making their way down to the lakeside to worship, to hunt, to live their precious lives.

I take a deep breath of this high air and can just smell the sea on the edge of it. A curlew is calling from somewhere nearby. A buzzard is mewling, a kestrel is hunting in the next field along. I leave the bench, turn, climb up and over the top of the valley.

# About the Author

Wendy Pratt is a poet, author, editor and workshop facilitator living and working on the North Yorkshire coast, where she grew up. She is the author of five collections of poetry.

Her collection *When I Think of My Body as a Horse* won the Poetry Business Book and Pamphlet award in 2021. She is founder and editor in chief of *Spelt Magazine* and facilitates online and in-person writing courses and workshops.

# Acknowledgements

It feels like a lifetime ago that I began work on *The Ghost Lake*. This makes it difficult to thank everyone by name, because there have been so many people I have met along the way. If I ever spoke to you about the book and you responded in a positive way, if you encouraged me, if you said you'd want to read it, if you said we need more writers from non-traditional backgrounds, if you were someone who was excited for me, thank you.

I began my writing career in my thirties, drawn to poetry during a very difficult time. I began my reading career much earlier, when my mum first passed me a Read It Yourself book and told me to have a go. All creative writing comes first from reading and the realisation that books do not magically appear, that *someone* is writing the books you read. It takes courage to put yourself forward and be that writer, especially if you come from a background or community that cannot easily access or experience the creative arts. To the writers who came before me, thank you. You were the people I could *see* that encouraged me to *be*. I want to thank the library staff, all the library staff the world over. As a child I would take bags of books out of Scarborough library every week, hulking them back on the bus or the train. I was so anxious as a child and a teen that catching the bus was a traumatic experience, but for the love of books I would do it. You helped open the world to me when I struggled to leave my room.

I want to thank the historians, naturalists, geologists, record keepers, archaeologists, photographers. I also want to acknowledge the amateurs alongside the experts, the walkers, the people recording the intimacies of everyday life, the celebrators of landscape. You are the holders of stories, and so often many of you don't make it into the history books. Without you I would not have been able to research my own landscape and the people who lived here.

Without the support of family and friends I would have gotten nowhere. I must therefore specifically thank my mum, my mother-in-law and my aunty Mary who shared her stories, her knowledge, her wine and her photographs with me when I was trying to piece together my dad's childhood. Thanks also to my oldest friend, Cassandra, because so many of my best memories involve her. I want to thank my kind and thoughtful friend Amy and also Matt for always being excited for me, even when Amy was going through the toughest of times. I also want to thank my friend Charlotte Oliver, whose ability to keep up with me during cocktail hour, along with her cheerleading of my work, is so welcome.

There are so many people from the writing community that I would like to thank, too many to mention, but in particular Tanya Shadrick, Electra Rhodes, Nicola Chester, Helen Mort, Victoria Bennett and Polly Atkin, who are all people whose writing I admire so much and who, in various ways, have helped me to scaffold the potential of the book around my wobbly confidence.

I give heartfelt thanks to the Yorkshire Coast Stanza Group.

I always come away nourished from our Sunday meet ups and your continued support has meant the world to me.

Thank you also to the community of village dog walkers who asked after the book each time they saw me walking the old dog and thanks too to the old dog himself, Toby, who would never have read this, on account of being a dog. He died not long after I completed the manuscript. I wish I could tell him that when I was with him, I felt a part of his pack. He allowed me to see the world from a different, animal perspective, and I miss him dearly. My gait is ever so slightly lopsided without him.

Thank you to my co-editors at *Spelt* magazine, Steve Nash and Helen Dewbery, whose support around the magazine, and also on a personal level, has meant the world to me, and to the contributors and columnists who have opened a whole other nature writing world to me and trusted me with their poetry and creative non-fiction.

Thanks also to the Nan Shepherd Prize judges who first longlisted the partial manuscript of *The Ghost Lake* and allowed me to believe I might take the book further, and to the Alpine Fellowship Award who shortlisted an essay that went on to be a chapter in this book.

Writing a book is a collaborative process, and I am so grateful for the team that worked with me to lift it out of my head and into a dust jacket. Thanks to my agent, Caro Clarke at Portobello Literary, who is precise, efficient, bold and caring all at once. She has been there to cheer me on, even before she was my agent. I am so glad to have had you by my side through this process. Thanks to everyone at The Borough Press, HarperCollins but in particular to Sophia Schoepfer, whose careful editing, gentle handling of difficult subject matter and respect towards me as a writer ensured this book worked.

Thank you to the staff at Scarborough library and at the Scarborough Museums Trust and at the East Yorkshire Archives for helping me find what I needed while researching. Your passion for detail and research is a huge support for writers. And a heartfelt thank you to anyone who ever digitised documents and made them publicly available. If you are rural, poor and unable to travel, online digital repositories ensure that you are not marginalised.

Thank you to Professor Nicky Milner, whose experience working at Star Carr enhanced my knowledge and who allowed me to come to her office and try on Star Carr headdress replicas. A highlight of the book writing process. Also to Dr Charlotte Rowley and Dr Jess Bates whose knowledge, hospitality and enthusiasm are very appreciated.

Thank you also to Lindsey Tyson who welcomed me into her beautiful art studio.

Thank you to my dad, who will not read this now, which breaks my heart. He died during the writing of the book. I'd planned to interview him and gather all his stories, but I left it too late. He instilled in me a passion for my ancestry and for our farming heritage. He is missed.

To the people who broke my heart along the way, to the people who said I couldn't and who said I shouldn't and who commented on my accent, or mocked the town where I grew up, you fuelled my fire, and should be thanked also.

Mostly I want to thank my husband, Chris Pratt, who never once told me to get a proper job. He is always my champion, always my safe place and my home.

Thank you.

# Bibliography

## Books

Mark Atherton, *Complete Old English: Teach Yourself* (Teach Yourself, London, 2019)

Margaret Atwood, *Negotiating with the Dead* (Cambridge University Press, Cambridge, 2002)

Andy Burnham (ed) *The Old Stones* (Watkins, London, 2018)

Rotha Mary Clay, *The Mediaeval Hospitals of England* (Methuen & Co, London, 1909)

Mark Cocker, *One Midsummer's Day* (Random House, London, 2023)

John Foggin, *Pressed for Time* (Calder Valley Press, 2022)

Helen Frisby, *Traditions of Death and Burial* (Shire Library, London, 2019)

Duncan Garrow and Neil Wilkin, *The World of Stone Henge*, (The British Museum, London, 2022)

William Greenwell, *British Barrows, a Record of the Examination of Sepulchral Mounds in Various Parts of Britain* (Clarendon Press, Oxford, 1877)

Thomas Hinderwell, *The History and Antiquities of Scarborough, and the Vicinity* (Thomas Wilson and Son, York, 1811)

Robert Hosfield, *The Earliest Europeans* (Oxbow Books, Oxford, 2020)

Amy Jeffs, *Wild* (Riverrun, London, 2021)

Kevin Leahy and Michael Lewis, *Finds Identified: Portable Antiquities Scheme* (Greenlight Publishing, Ipswich, 2018)

Hilary Mantel, *Bring up the Bodies*, (Fourth Estate, 2012) p. 334

Nicky Milner et al, *Star Carr Volume 1: A Persistent Place in a Changing World* (White Rose University Press, York, 2018)

Nicky Milner et al, *Star Carr Volume 2: Studies in Technology, Subsistence and Environment* (White Rose University Press, York, 2018)

Nicky Milner et al, *Star Carr: Life in Britain after the Ice Age* (Council for British Archaeology, York, 2013)

Eliza Ann Harris Dick Ogilvy and Robert Ronald McLan, *A Book of Highland Minstrelsy* (T Bosworth, London, 1818)

D.J. Palmer, 'The Early Comedies', in Stanley Wells (ed.), *Shakespeare: A Bibliographical Guide* (Oxford University Press, Oxford, 1992), pp. 83–105

D. Powlesland, *The Heslerton Anglo Saxon Settlement: A Guide to the Excavation of an Early Anglo-Saxon Settlement and its Cemetery* (North Yorkshire County Council, Northallerton, 1987)

Annie Proulx, *Fen, Bog and Swamp* (HarperCollins, London, 2022)

Peter J. Reynold, *Ancient Farming* (Shire Publications, Risborough, 2011)

Alice Roberts, *Ancestors* (Simon & Schuster, London, 2021)

Ian Rotherham, *Yorkshire's Forgotten Fens* (Wharncliffe Books, Barnsley, 2010)

Nan Shepherd, *The Living Mountain* (Canongate Books, Edinburgh, 1996)

Rebecca Smith, *Rural* (William Collins, Glasgow, 2023)

William Smithson, *An Historical and Descriptive Guide to Filey* (Matthew Turner Kendall, Filey, 1861)

Joseph Strutt, *The Sports and Pastimes of the People of England* Including the *Rural and Domestic Recreations, May Games, Mummeries, Shows, Processions, Pageants, and Pompous Spectacles from the Earliest Period to the Present Time* (Methuen & Company, London, 1801)

Christopher Tilley, *A Phenomenology of Landscape: Places, Paths and Monuments* (Berg Publishers, Oxford, 1994)

Peter N. Walker, *Murders and Mysteries from the North York Moors* (Robert Hale, London, 1988)

## Articles and Journals

Ammar Azzouz and Pippa Catterall, 'Most Public Spaces Are Male Spaces', *The Developer,* (Online, 20 May 2021)

T.C.M. Brewster, 'Two Bronze Age Barrows in the North Riding of Yorkshire', *Yorkshire Archaeological Journal,* (Vol. 45, The Yorkshire Archaeological Society, Leeds, 1973) pp. 55-96

A.D. Conningham, 'Account of Discoveries made in Barrows Near Scarborough', *Journal of the British Archaeology Association* (1848)

David Coombs, 'The Excavation of Two Bronze Age Round Barrows on Irton Moor, Yorks. 1973', *Yorkshire Archaeological Journal,* Vol. 66 (1994) pp. 21-50

Simon Fairlie, 'A Short History of Enclosure in Britain', *The Land,* 7 (Summer 2009) pp. 16-31

Pam Graves, 'Canon William Greenwell and His Contemporaries: The History of British Archaeology in the Nineteenth and Early Twentieth Centuries', *Bulletin of the History of Archaeology*, 15 (2), pp. 45-49

Lucy Jones, 'The new science of motherhood shows it's far more transformative than western culture allows', *Guardian* (30 July 2023)

D. D. A. Simpson, A. M. Gibson, G. Malazarte-Smith (with contributions by), Carole Keepax & SusanLimbrey (20 15) The Excavation of Barrow III, Irton Moor, North Yorkshire, *Yorkshire Archaeological Journal*, 87:1, pp. 11-36

**Websites**

ArchaeologyFollow, University of York. 'Star Carr Frontlet 115876.' *Sketchfab*, 1 Jan. 1965, sketchfab.com/3d-models/star-carr-frontlet-115876-0c0c2bb06adf-476c842b5e8dbd6031fe.

*Bridlington Priory*, bridlingtonpriory.co.uk/history-of-bridlington-priory/.

'Diederik Knapping Flint.' *YouTube*, YouTube, 31 May 2019, www.youtube.com/watch?v=NH6Vxum3AVI.

'Folkton, Yorkshire, England. Geographical and Historical Information from 1868., Yorkshire (East Riding).' *Genuki*, www.genuki.org.uk/big/eng/YKS/ERY/Folkton/Folkton68.

'Great Wolf Slayers of England.' *Historic UK*, 17 Nov. 2023, www.historic-uk.com/HistoryUK/HistoryofEngland/Great-Wolf-Slayers-Of-England/.

'Historic England Research Records.' *Heritage Gateway*, www.heritagegateway.org.uk/Gateway/Results_Single.aspx?uid=2435d4c0-4ef2-4820-a0c2-c4a97f890b2e&resourceID=19191.

'History of the Society.' *Scarborough Archaeological Society*

| *History of the Society*, www.sahs.org.uk/history-of-the-society.html.

'Hospitals: Crayke - Hedon.' *Hospitals: Crayke - Hedon | British History Online*, www.british-history.ac.uk/vch/yorks/vol3/pp306-310#fnn36.

'Hospitals: Scarborough - Yarm.' *Hospitals: Scarborough - Yarm | British History Online*, www.british-history.ac.uk/vch/yorks/vol3/pp330-336.

'Hunmanby.' *Wikipedia*, Wikimedia Foundation, 12 Feb. 2024, en.wikipedia.org/wiki/Hunmanby.

'Monasticon Anglicanum, or, the History of the Ancient Abbies, and Other Monasteries, Hospitals, Cathedral and Collegiate Churches in England and Wales. with Divers French, Irish, and Scotch Monasteries Formerly Relating to England: Dugdale, William, Sir.' *Internet Archive*, Sam Keble; Hen. Rhodes, 1 Jan. 1693, archive.org/details/monasticonanglic00dugd/page/176/mode/2up.

'Project Gutenberg's The Mediæval Hospitals of England, by Rotha Mary Clay.' *Project Gutenberg*, www.gutenberg.org/files/50501/50501-h/50501-h.htm#fn_3.

Reppion, John. 'The Last Wolf in England.' *The Daily Grail*, 15 Dec. 2019, www.dailygrail.com/2019/12/the-last-wolf-in-england/.

'Star Carr Archives Project.' *Archaeology Data Service*, archaeologydataservice.ac.uk/archives/view/scarr_eh_2013/query.cfm.

'Thomas Hinderwell.' *Wikipedia*, Wikimedia Foundation, 15 Aug. 2022, en.wikipedia.org/wiki/Thomas_Hinderwell.

'Tom Lord Talking about Tot Lord Visiting Star Carr.' *YouTube*, YouTube, 23 May 2019, www.youtube.com/watch?v=tnQfTE3xGs8.

*Wendy Pratt*

'Transactions of the Scarborough Archaeological and Historical Society No. 27 : Scarborough Archaeological and Historical Society.' *Internet Archive*, 1 Jan. 1989, archive.org/details/scarborough026.

'Welcome to CalmView.' *Archives Catalogue - East Riding of Yorkshire Council*, calmview.eastriding.gov.uk/.